T0224072

Communications in Computer and Information Science   **1020**

Commenced Publication in 2007
Founding and Former Series Editors:
Phoebe Chen, Alfredo Cuzzocrea, Xiaoyong Du, Orhun Kara, Ting Liu,
Krishna M. Sivalingam, Dominik Ślęzak, Takashi Washio, and Xiaokang Yang

More information about this series at http://www.springer.com/series/7899

Suresh Sundaram · Gaurav Harit (Eds.)

Document Analysis and Recognition

4th Workshop, DAR 2018
Held in Conjunction with ICVGIP 2018
Hyderabad, India, December 18, 2018
Revised Selected Papers

Springer

Editors
Suresh Sundaram
Electronics and Electrical Engineering
Indian Institute of Technology Guwahati
Guwahati, India

Gaurav Harit
Computer Science and Engineering
Indian Institute of Technology Jodhpur
Karwar, Rajasthan, India

ISSN 1865-0929   ISSN 1865-0937 (electronic)
Communications in Computer and Information Science
ISBN 978-981-13-9360-0   ISBN 978-981-13-9361-7 (eBook)
https://doi.org/10.1007/978-981-13-9361-7

This Springer imprint is published by the registered company Springer Nature Singapore Pte Ltd.
The registered company address is: 152 Beach Road, #21-01/04 Gateway East, Singapore 189721, Singapore

Preface

The 4th Workshop on Document Analysis and Recognition (DAR 2018) was held at Hyderabad, Telangana, India, on December 18, 2018. This edition was organized by the International Institute of Information Technology, Hyderabad (IIIT-H) as part of the 11th Indian Conference on Vision, Graphics, and Image Processing (ICVGIP 2018). The DAR workshop series brings together researchers working in the area of document analysis, with the focus of exchanging ideas in order to foster further research in the field. The present proceedings contain the papers that were accepted and presented at the workshop.

Broadly speaking, the papers presented in this volume describe developments in different facets of document analysis, such as:

(a) Document layout analysis and understanding
(b) Handwriting recognition and symbol spotting
(c) Character and word segmentation
(d) Handwriting analysis
(e) Datasets and performance evaluation

From a total of 22 papers submitted to the workshop, a total of 14 were accepted and presented. The papers were selected based on three reviews obtained for each of the submissions. Members of the Program Committee were involved in the review of the papers, for which a single-blinded procedure was adopted. The papers in the proceedings are the revised versions that were submitted after the incorporation of the reviewer comments. Apart from paper presentations, the workshop also hosted a keynote talk by Prof. A. G. Ramakrishnan, Department of Electrical Engineering, Indian Institute of Science, Bangalore.

June 2019

Suresh Sundaram
Gaurav Harit

Organization

Advisory Committee

Bidyut Baran Chaudhuri	ISI Kolkata, India
Santanu Chaudhury	CSIR-CEERI and IIT Delhi, India
Umapada Pal	ISI Kolkata, India
Angarai Ganesan Ramakrishnan	IISc Bangalore, India

Program Co-chairs

Suresh Sundaram	IIT Guwahati, India
Gaurav Harit	IIT Jodhpur, India

Program Committee

Ujjwal Bhattacharya	ISI Kolkata, India
Utpal Garain	ISI Kolkata, India
Prithwijit Guha	IIT Guwahati, India
D. S. Guru	University of Mysore, India
Thotreingam Kasar	Kaaya Tech, India
Gurpreet Singh Lehal	Panjab University, India
Anand Mishra	IISc Bangalore, India
Atul Negi	University of Hyderabad, India
Swapan Parui	ISI Kolkata, India
Shivakumara Palaiahnakote	University of Malaya, Malaysia
Sitaram Ramachandrula	DXC Technology, India
Partha Pratim Roy	IIT Roorkee, India
Rajendra Kumar Sharma	Thapar Institute of Engineering and Technology, India
Kiran Hiremath	IIT Jodhpur, India
Yashaswi Verma	IIT Jodhpur, India
Abhishek Sharma	IIIT Naya Raipur, India
A. V. Narasimhadhan	NIT Karnataka, India
Ayesha Choudhury	Jawaharlal Nehru University, India

Contents

Document Layout Analysis and Understanding

MultiDIAS: A Hierarchical Multi-layered Document Image Annotation System

Arnab Poddar$^{(\boxtimes)}$, Rohan Mukherjee, Jayanta Mukhopadhyay,
and Prabir Kumar Biswas

Indian Institute of Technology Kharagpur, Kharagpur, India
arnab.poddar91@gmail.com

Abstract. Content of the document images are often shows hierarchical multi-layered tree structure. Further, the algorithms for document image applications like line detection, paragraph detection, word recognition, layout analysis etc. require pixel level annotation. In this paper, a Multi-layered Document Image Annotation System (MultiDIAS) has been introduced. The proposed system simultaneously provide a platform for hierarchical and pixel level annotation of document. MultiDIAS label the document image in four hierarchical layers (layout type, entity type, line type, word type) assigned by the user. The output generated are four ground-truth images and an XML file representing the metadata information. The MultiDIAS is tested on a complex handwritten manuscript written by renowned film director Satyajit Ray for the movie 'Goopi Gyne Bagha Byne'. This annotated data generated using Multi-DIAS can further be used in a wide range of applications of document image understanding and analysis.

Keywords: Document image analysis · Pixel-level annotation · Hierarchical annotation

1 Introduction

The last two decades have witnessed a rapid rise in the requirement of digitization of documents and the availability of several text-based softwares has enlarged the scope of analysis of such documents. Several document image analysis methodologies are widely used to generate outputs in the machine readable format from raw content [1]. The different phases of a document analysis system include scanning, segmentation and layout analysis, logical structure and semantic analysis, article and content extraction, and re-purposing of the extracted information into other application specific formats [1].

Typical document image analysis includes document layout analysis, optical character recognition, biometric identity detection from signatures or handwriting and graphical object recognition. Various methodologies have been introduced and experimented to handle the objectives related to the application of

© Springer Nature Singapore Pte Ltd. 2019
S. Sundaram and G. Harit (Eds.): DAR 2018, CCIS 1020, pp. 3–14, 2019.
https://doi.org/10.1007/978-981-13-9361-7_1

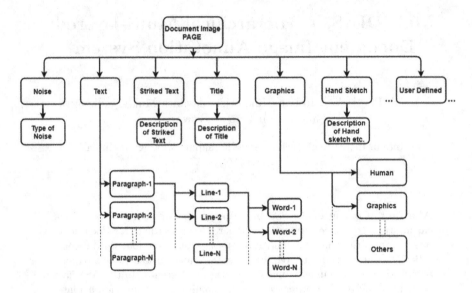

Fig. 1. Multi-layered hierarchical information based representation of a typical document image for annotation.

document images [1,11]. The performance metrics of the algorithms are evaluated considering the ground-truth of the acquired document image data. The data with corresponding ground-truth has substantial significance in document image analysis. The generation of ground-truth is a rigorous manual process that needs significant time and effort from the user. Hence, the system for generating ground-truth requires an user-friendly, convenient and efficient environment which is capable of delivering reliable ground-truth data.

Various systems for ground-truth generation have been proposed in relevant literature to prepare benchmark database for the evaluation of designed algorithms. Pink Panther [21] was introduced as a ground-truth generator which is predominantly used for the annotation of document images to evaluate the algorithms for layout analysis. A system named PerfectDoc [19] is used especially for layout structures of the document images. The authors in [9,15,20] have presented Various layout based ground-truth generation tools. The ground-truth generators in [9,17,19] can only allow rectangular bounding-boxes for annotation. Thus their performances degenerate in case of documents with complex layout. A recent ground-truth generator GEDI [5] supports annotation by generating a polygonal region. However, it is observed that the tool is quite inefficient for images of larger dimension (600dpi). A Pixel level ground-truth generator named PixLabeler has been reported in [13]. Similar tools are also referred in [10,14,18]. Of late, a web based document image annotation tool for correction of pixel-label is proposed in [12]. Pixel level annotation contains more specific information but it costs higher time requirement for execution of the assigned task.

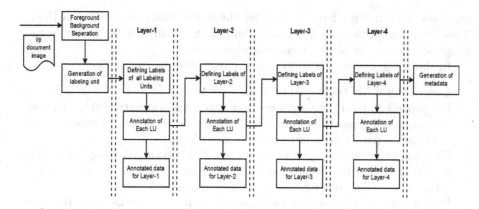

Fig. 2. Block diagram for different layer annotation with MultiDIAS system

The state-of-the-art annotation tools use pixel label annotation process for more precise ground-truth generation [13]. The pixel-level annotation in multiple layers will not only allow to evaluate techniques for layout analysis but also help to deal with other problems like word spotting, paragraph detection, line detection, detection of types and entities of the graphical contents. Hence, an ideal ground-truth generation interface should feature the characteristics to handle multi-layered hierarchical information and simultaneously pursue precise pixel-level annotation. However, as pixel level annotation is a rigorous process, the system should be fast and user-friendly.

In this paper, we propose a semi-supervised graphical-user-interface (GUI) for ground-truth generation tool called Multi-layered Document Image Annotation System (MultiDIAS). A pictorial representation of the hierarchical information contained in typical documents is depicted in Fig. 1. The proposed system can accommodate the multi-layered structure of the information content of the document images and simultaneously provide a simple platform to allow pixel level annotation of document images in various layers. A block level depiction of various modules of the MultiDIAS system is given in Fig. 2. It generates an XML file consisting of the metadata information, along with four layered ground-truth images. In our present implementation of MultiDIAS, only single annotation label per block/pixel is accommodated. MultiDIAS enables a researcher in the field of document image processing to evaluate different algorithms for a wide range of problems on the same document image data. Various approaches proposed to handle the problems like layout analysis, word detection, line detection, paragraph detection, graphical entity recognition can be evaluated with the same document image data using the introduced MultiDIAS toolkit. In general, the document image layouts are well structured in case of printed documents. However, in handwritten documents, especially in manuscripts, the information content are presented with higher complexity. The proposed MultiDIAS in designed for application on both printed and handwritten document images for annotation. The MultiDIAS is tested on a complex handwritten manuscript written by renowned film director Satyajit Ray for the movie 'Goopi Gyne Bagha Byne'. This annotated data generated using MultiDIAS can further be used in a wide range of applications of document image analysis.

In short, the major contribution of the paper can be summarized as

- A hierarchical Multi-layer Annotation System is proposed.
- The proposed system can accommodate hierarchical structure of information content of the typical document images and the proposed architecture provides each separate layer annotation in pixel-level.
- The algorithms for multiple problems like line detection, paragraph detection, word recognition, layout analysis can be evaluated on same document image data using the ground-truth, generated by proposed system.
- The system incorporates semi-automatic approach for labeling the foreground pixels.
- The tool presents a meta-data of the relation of the fore-ground pixels in different layers in XML.

The basic system architecture of MultiDIAS is presented in Sect. 2. The functionality of the proposed system is described in Sect. 3. Implementation details are discussed in Sects. 4 and 5 depicts the details of ground-truth generation with MultiDIAS. Finally, we conclude in Sect. 6.

2   System Architecture of Multi-DIAS

In general, the information in both hand-written or printed document images contain one or more paragraphs, the paragraphs contain one or more text lines and each text line contains multiple words. On the other hand, the non-text regions may contain graphics, header, hand-sketch, striked-text, etc. A block level representation of the hierarchical information contained in a typical document is presented in Fig. 1.

Here we aim to provide annotation of hierarchical information at different layers and simultaneously present a platform to generate pixel level annotation in each layer. A block diagram of different modules of the MultiDIAS system is presented in Fig. 2. Initially, the pre-processing steps are conducted. The foreground pixels, required to be annotated, are obtained through the pre-processing operations. Henceforth, the foreground pixels are transformed into labeling units for further annotation.

In MultiDIAS, all the foreground pixels are initially labeled in the first layer as text, graphics, hand-sketch, page number, header, bold-text, etc. in accordance with the page-layout. Each individual label in the first layer can be subdivided into multiple sub-labels in the next layer. For example, the text region labeled in the first layer can be sub-divided into multiple paragraphs in the second layer. Moreover, the pixels labeled as graphics in the first layer can be sub-divided into hand-drawn sketch, human figure, animal figure, etc. in the second layer. The document image pixels with graphical content can be accommodated in three layers as **Graphics → Entity → instances**. The text pixels

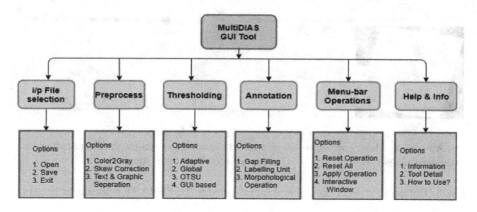

Fig. 3. Block diagram showing multiple features of preprocessing steps and annotation process with MultiDIAS system.

(a) Converting the input im- (b) Operation of Threshold- (c) Gap filling of the thresh-
age to gray-scale image.   ing using GUI.   olded image using GUI.

Fig. 4. Different stages of annotated images at multiple layers of a document image. This is a page of manuscript of the movie Goopi Gyne Bagha Byne, directed and scripted by Satyajit Ray

can be accommodated up-to word level in 4 layers as shown in Fig. 6a (**Text** →
Paragraphs → **Lines** → **Word**). In MultiDIAS, the annotation of the labeling units can be done up-to 4 distinct layers, each in pixel level. In the initial
layer (Layer-1), the annotation of the basic layout of the page can be accommodated. Subsequently in second layer, the objects of each distinct label assigned
in Layer-1 can be annotated as per requirement into multiple sub-labels. This
process is extended similarly for layer-3 and layer-4 as shown in Fig. 2. Finally,
four ground-truth images are generated along with a tree, showing the metadata
of the labels at multiple layers.

3   Functionality

This section discusses the different operations and tasks associated with the
proposed MultiDIAS system. Figure 3 presents a summary.

(a) Automatic Skew correction of printed document image.

(b) Automatic text-graphics separation on printed document images.

Fig. 5. Different preprocessing operation provided in MultiDIAS for document images.

3.1 Preprocessing

In the proposed MultiDIAS annotation system, the user is allowed to segment the foreground opting either of the four thresholding choices- GUI-based thresholding, a GUI-based adaptive thresholding, the Otsu's thresholding and the global thresholding technique [7]. A typical view of foreground separation module carried out with the GUI-based thresholding choice is displayed in Fig. 4b. Moreover, for printed document images, MultiDIAS provides an in-built platform for skew-angle correction operation as in [2]. It also provides the user the option to separate the text and graphics part automatically. Figure 5a and b display an example for skew correction and separation of texts and graphics respectively in document images of Indian language (Bengali).

3.2 Editing the Binary Image

In the proposed MultiDIAS system, the user is allowed to edit the foreground pixels and avoid the overlapping of labeling unit. Through the semi-automatic approach incorporated in the tool to separate the foreground and background pixels, the user can precisely edit the foreground pixels by visual inspection. Using this option, one can accurately segment the overlapping labeling units.

3.3 Generation of Labeling Unit

MultiDIAS incorporates a approach for pre-defining the Labeling Units (LU). This is done using GUI based Morphological operations like dilation, erosion, opening, closing, smoothing and gap-filling that have been included in Multi-DIAS for generation of LUs. An LU indicates a defined set of pixels from foreground, assigned together as a unit by an appropriate morphological operator. Pixels are clustered together by selecting either of the morphological operations - opening, closing, dilation, and erosion [7].

The annotator is supposed to choose an element of suitable size and element type using the graphical slider provided in the GUI of MultiDIAS, for grouping

Algorithm 1. Label all *LU* in *Layer*

Require: $\forall labellist \neq NULL; labellist \in LabelList$
  $LabelList \leftarrow NULL$
  $Objects \leftarrow$ all uniquely labeled Objects in $Layer - 1$
  $LU[Object] \leftarrow$ valid unlabeled units $\forall Object \in Objects$
  $Label \leftarrow$ NULL
  while $Label[LU[Object]] \neq NULL : \forall Object \in Objects$ **do**
    $SU \leftarrow NULL$
    $[X, Y] \leftarrow$ Select RoI from USER
    while $Label[lu] \neq NULL : \forall lu \in LU$ **do**
      if Boundingbox$(lu) \leq [X, Y]$ **then**
        $SU \leftarrow lu \cup SU$
      end if
    end while
    $label =$Mention Label for RoI from USER
    if $label \notin Label$ **then**
      $LabelList \leftarrow label \cup LabelList$
    end if
    $Label[SU] \leftarrow label$
  end while

---

pixels. A user can perform morphological operations on pixels to form the labeling units by a smoothing operation, where the selection of run length parameter is done interactively. Moreover, the foreground pixels are allowed to be accumulated together using the morphological operations like gap-filling [4]. Here, the selection of the input parameters, gap size in vertical and horizontal directions are taken as inputs from the user as per requirement using the designed GUI. A graphical instance of MultiDIAS for performing the operation is displayed in Fig. 4c.

After grouping operation on the foreground pixels, all the contours of the groups are estimated adopting the technique proposed in [16]. Subsequently, the estimated contours are approximated as a polygon using Douglas-Peucker algorithm [6]. These computed polygons are considered as the elemental labeling units for annotation in MultiDIAS in different layers. An example of a collection of labeling units is shown in Fig. 6, where each unit is highlighted using a unique color.

3.4 Label Definition

There are a few pre-defined key-labels provided in MultiDIAS in different layers. The tool facilitates an option to add and label as per requirement as shown in Fig. 6a. A user can annotate the labeling units of the input document with the existing labels with unique identification number and can also add labels simultaneously at the time of annotation.

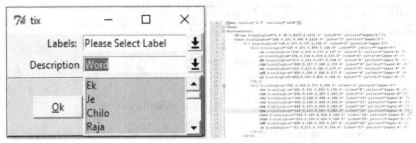

(a) Dialog box showing labels to be given as inputs in the different layers in MultiDIAS system. Here the dialog box for label input in 4th layer is shown, where the different words are being annotated corresponding to line-1 of paragraph-1 of text.

(b) An example of the generated XML file is presented. The above XML file is generated using the page presented in Figure. 6.

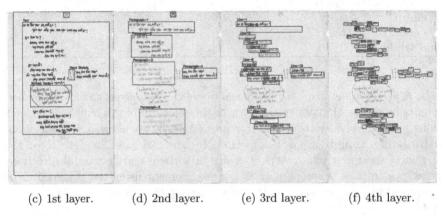

(c) 1st layer.   (d) 2nd layer.   (e) 3rd layer.   (f) 4th layer.

Fig. 6. Different stages of an annotated document image at multiple layers. The image is a manuscript from the movie 'Goopi Gyne Bagha Byne', directed and scripted by *Satyajit Ray*

3.5 Annotation of LUs in Different Layers

The comprehensive annotation process taking place across multiple layers is depicted as Algorithm 1. In each layer, the annotation of labeling units (LUs) is executed by selecting a region of interest (ROI). At first, all the units are determined which are completely present within the selected ROI. After selection of a ROI, all the unlabeled units present in it can be labeled using two different modes. A user gets to annotate all units within the ROI with label from the present list. These LUs, as selected from user-given ROI, will be added to set of LUs, assigned to previously defined labels. Otherwise, the user can add a new label by naming it in the dialog-box appearing in MultiDIAS. This will update all the unlabeled units with the label given by the user. The pixel-color

Table 1. Comparison of features of different annotation systems

	Handles hierarchical information	Metadata of relation between pixels	Open source	Free to use	Batch label	Handles large images	Pixel-level	Independent from pre-processed input
MultiDIAS	Yes	Yes	Yes	Yes	Yes	Yes	Yes	Yes
Pixel.js [12]	No	No	Yes	Yes	Yes	Yes	Yes	Yes
Pix-Labler [13]	No	No	No	Yes	Yes	Yes	Yes	No
DivaDia [3]	No	No	Yes	Yes	Yes	No	No	Yes
Picozu[a]	No	No	No	Yes	No	No	Yes	Yes

[a]https://www.picozu.com/.

of those regions are set to the color of that label. Reference of a particular pixel to a given labeling unit is enumerated by point-polygon test [8]. At every phase of the annotation of a particular layer, the MultiDIAS shows revised color image, where the labeled pixels are exhibited with the color of the corresponding label, and the unlabeled pixels are displayed with the original value of the pixel. The process of annotation continues until all labeling units are marked. After completion of annotation of each layer, the annotated image is displayed with bounding boxes for all distinct labels.

A similar process of annotation is followed for all the four layers in Multi-DIAS. Once the labeling procedure of a particular layer is completed, the MultiDIAS system automatically moves to its next layer for annotation. In a higher layer of annotation, a set of labeling units assigned to a particular label in previous layer are allowed to be sub-divided into multiple sub-labels in the present layer as required. If there is no need to sub-divide a particular label in the previous layer, the user can choose 'None' label in the present layer. Those labeling units marked as 'None' in a particular layer will not appear further in the higher layers as per the design of MultiDIAS system presented in Algorithm 1.

All distinct labels of the previous layers are treated one-by-one separately, showing a bounding-box and highlighting the assigned labeling units for each label. This process is followed hierarchically in every layers. On completion of annotation of each layers, the annotated ground-truth image is generated by MultiDIAS for the particular label.

After finalizing the four layers (Layer-1: Fig. 6c, Layer-2: Fig. 6d, Layer-3: Fig. 6e, Layer-4: Fig. 6f), output labeled image and its corresponding XML file are generated in tree format. An example of different stages of labeling is shown in Fig. 6.

3.6 Representation of the Annotated Data in XML Format

Finally, the metadata of the document image is presented in XML format. The system creates a tree structure representing the four layers in four different levels. Every element in each layer contains 4 attributes, namely, (i) name of node, (ii) bounding box, (iii) label number, (iv) layer number.

The name of the node is assigned by the dialog-box as shown in Fig. 6a. The parameters of the bounding box is automatically measured by calculating all the labeling units, fully accommodated within the region of interest given by the user. The bounding-box in the nodes is parameterized as x-coordinate, y-coordinate, stretch in x-dimension, stretch in y-dimension. The label number denotes a unique integer number which is used to denote the corresponding label in the pixels of ground-truth image. For each particular layer, the label numbers are set uniquely. Finally, the layer number is attributed with each node. It varies from 1 to 4.

4   Implementation Details

MultiDIAS is implemented in Python 2.7 environment, using graphical user interface and with customizable standard modules, developed using OpenCV [7]. The annotation process of a document image is conducted through the graphical user interface, provided in MultiDIAS and subsequently, a ground-truth image in '.png' format is generated in each of the four layers of annotation. Each of the pixels of the ground-truth images are represented with an index corresponding to a particular label of annotation. The hierarchical metadata of the document image, under consideration is saved in '.XML ' format, which also comprises of the information of the original image along with the annotated ground-truth images of four layers.

In the XML file, an index of a layer corresponds to the unique pixel value for a particular label in the ground-truth image of the corresponding layer. As an example, annotated images in four different hierarchical layers are shown in Fig. 6c–f respectively. MultiDIAS is tested to annotate images from the scanned handwritten document images taken the hand-written scripts of renowned film-maker Satyajit Ray. The manuscripts were created for his famous movie 'Goopi Gyne Bagha Byne'.

5   Generation of Ground-Truth with MultiDIAS

MultiDIAS is used to generate ground-truth for the complex hand-written manuscript documents of Satyajit Ray. The images in the hand-written manuscripts consist of a wide range of regions like page numbers, text, bold-texts, headers, signatures, hand-sketches, headlines other foot notes, lines, indicators. The orientation of the documents also varies randomly. Moreover, in handwritten documents the lines, paragraphs etc. are non-uniformly skewed. The number of labels in the other layers depends on the paragraphs, lines, number of words, types of sketches etc. in the manuscript images. The time of the other layers depends on the content of particular document' s lines, sketches, words etc. A comparative study of various features of the annotation tools between proposed system and other existing annotation tools are presented in Table 1. Approximate time taken by a user for annotation of 1-st layer of a typical document image with MultiDIAS is nearly 3–4 min.

6   Conclusion

The primary aim of MultiDIAS is to annotate an input document image with hierarchical information efficiently in a single platform. MultiDIAS enables a researcher in the field of document image processing to evaluate different algorithms for a wide range of problems on the same document image data. Various approaches proposed to handle the problems like layout analysis, word detection, line detection, paragraph detection, graphical entity recognition etc. can be evaluated with the same document image data using the introduced MultiDIAS toolkit. At the same time, MultiDIAS provides a user friendly simple platform to annotate hand-written and other document images efficiently in pixel level. MultiDIAS generates an '.XML' file consisting the metadata information, along with four layered ground-truth images. In our present implementation of MultiDIAS, only single annotation label per block/pixel is accommodated. In other situations, it is preferable to accommodate multiple annotations per block/pixels, especially in case of overlapping. In our future endeavor, we plan to address the limitation and incorporate more than one annotation per block. The authors expect that MultiDIAS can potentially serve the document image analysis community by simplifying the ground-truth generation procedure.

Acknowledgement. This research was partially supported and funded by IMPRINT, Government of India, through the research project titled "Information Access from Document Images of Indian Languages".

References

1. Bhowmik, S., Sarkar, R., Nasipuri, M., Doermann, D.: Text and non-text separation in offline document images: a survey. Int. J. Doc. Anal. Recognit. (IJDAR) **21**(1–2), 1–20 (2018)
2. Chaudhuri, B., Pal, U.: Skew angle detection of digitized indian script documents. IEEE Trans. Pattern Anal. Mach. Intell. **19**(2), 182–186 (1997)
3. Chen, K., Seuret, M., Wei, H., Liwicki, M., Hennebert, J., Ingold, R.: Ground truth model, tool, and dataset for layout analysis of historical documents. In: Document Recognition and Retrieval XXII, vol. 9402, p. 940204. International Society for Optics and Photonics (2015)
4. Dey, S., Mukherjee, J., Sural, S., Nandedkar, A.V.: Anveshak - a groundtruth generation tool for foreground regions of document images. In: Mukherjee, S., Mukherjee, S., Mukherjee, D.P., Sivaswamy, J., Awate, S., Setlur, S., Namboodiri, A.M., Chaudhury, S. (eds.) ICVGIP 2016. LNCS, vol. 10481, pp. 255–264. Springer, Cham (2017). https://doi.org/10.1007/978-3-319-68124-5_22
5. Doermann, D., Zotkina, E., Li, H.: GEDI-a groundtruthing environment for document images. In: Ninth IAPR International Workshop on Document Analysis Systems (DAS 2010). Citeseer (2010)
6. Douglas, D.H., Peucker, T.K.: Algorithms for the reduction of the number of points required to represent a digitized line or its caricature. Cartographica: Int. J. Geog. Inf. Geovisualization **10**(2), 112–122 (1973)
7. Gonzalez, R.C., Woods, R.E., et al.: Digital image processing (2002)

8. Hormann, K., Agathos, A.: The point in polygon problem for arbitrary polygons. Comput. Geometry **20**(3), 131–144 (2001)
9. Lee, C.H., Kanungo, T.: The architecture of trueviz: a groundtruth/metadata editing and visualizing toolkit. Pattern Recognit. **36**(3), 811–825 (2003)
10. Moll, M.A., Baird, H.S., An, C.: Truthing for pixel-accurate segmentation. In: The Eighth IAPR International Workshop on Document Analysis Systems, pp. 379–385. IEEE (2008)
11. Pal, U., Chaudhuri, B.: Indian script character recognition: a survey. Pattern Recognit. **37**(9), 1887–1899 (2004)
12. Saleh, Z., Zhang, K., Calvo-Zaragoza, J., Vigliensoni, G., Fujinaga, I.: Pixel. js: web-based pixel classification correction platform for ground truth creation. In: 2017 14th IAPR International Conference on Document Analysis and Recognition (ICDAR), vol. 2, pp. 39–40. IEEE (2017)
13. Saund, E., Lin, J., Sarkar, P.: Pixlabeler: user interface for pixel-level labeling of elements in document images. In: 10th International Conference on Document Analysis and Recognition, ICDAR 2009, pp. 646–650. IEEE (2009)
14. Shafait, F., Keysers, D., Breuel, T.M.: Pixel-accurate representation and evaluation of page segmentation in document images, pp. 872–875. IEEE (2006)
15. Strecker, T., Van Beusekom, J., Albayrak, S., Breuel, T.M.: Automated ground truth data generation for newspaper document images. In: 10th International Conference on Document Analysis and Recognition, ICDAR 2009, pp. 1275–1279. IEEE (2009)
16. Suzuki, S., et al.: Topological structural analysis of digitized binary images by border following. Comput. Vis. Graph. Image Process. **30**(1), 32–46 (1985)
17. Thoma, G.: Ground truth data for document image analysis. In: Symposium on Document Image Understanding and Technology (SDIUT), pp. 199–205 (2003)
18. Wenyin, L., Dori, D.: A protocol for performance evaluation of line detection algorithms. Mach. Vis. Appl. **9**(5–6), 240–250 (1997)
19. Yacoub, S., Saxena, V., Sami, S.N.: Perfectdoc: a ground truthing environment for complex documents. In: Proceedings of the Eighth International Conference on Document Analysis and Recognition, pp. 452–456. IEEE (2005)
20. Yang, L., Huang, W., Tan, C.L.: Semi-automatic ground truth generation for chart image recognition. In: Bunke, H., Spitz, A.L. (eds.) DAS 2006. LNCS, vol. 3872, pp. 324–335. Springer, Heidelberg (2006). https://doi.org/10.1007/11669487_29
21. Yanikoglu, B.A., Vincent, L.: Pink panther: a complete environment for ground-truthing and benchmarking document page segmentation. Pattern Recognit. **31**(9), 1191–1204 (1998)

Attributed Paths for Layout-Based Document Retrieval

Divya Sharma, Gaurav Harit$^{(\boxtimes)}$, and Chiranjoy Chattopadhyay

Department of Computer Science and Engineering,
Indian Institute of Technology Jodhpur, Jodhpur, India
{sharma.12,gharit,chiranjoy}@iitj.ac.in

Abstract. A document is rich in its layout. The entities of interest can be scattered over the document page. Traditional layout matching has involved modeling layout structure as grids, graphs, and spatial histograms of patches. In this paper we propose a new way of representing layout, which we call *attributed paths*. This representation admits a string edit distance based match measure. Our experiments show that layout based retrieval using attributed paths is computationally efficient and more effective. It also offers flexibility in tuning the match criterion. We have demonstrated effectiveness of attributed paths in performing layout based retrieval tasks on datasets of floor plan images [14] and journal pages [1].

1 Introduction

Document layout analysis deals with decomposing a given document image into its component regions and understanding their functional roles and relationships. A document image is composed of a variety of physical entities or regions such as text blocks, lines, words, figures, tables, and background. Functional or logical labels such as sentences, titles, captions, author names, and address, can be assigned to some of these regions. Document image classification and retrieval, is a crucial step in any digital mailroom scenario, and is one of the most explored topics that involve document layout analysis. The problem of retrieving similar document images to a given query has been tackled from different angles, mainly depending on what is understood as the notion of similarity between documents. In each scenario, depending on the user expectations, the document images can be represented and described by three broad families of descriptors: textual content, visual appearance, and layout structure.

1.1 Document Layout Features

Document features can be of different types, for example, image features, extracted directly from the image or from a segmented image (e.g. the density of black pixels of a region), structural features or relationships between blocks in the page, obtained from the page layout, and textual features, based

S. Sundaram and G. Harit (Eds.): DAR 2018, CCIS 1020, pp. 15–26, 2019.
https://doi.org/10.1007/978-981-13-9361-7_2

on the OCR output of the image. Out of these three, structural features are necessary to classify documents with layout structure variations. Authors in [15] propose the use of maximal grid of the frameset in documents. A scanned image of a form document is processed to extract the cells and a maximal grid is then obtained. This grid encompasses all the horizontal and vertical lines in the form and is generated using the cell coordinates. The number of cells from the original frameset, included in each of the cells created by the maximal grid, is then calculated. The counts of these cells are then added for each row and column to generate an array representation for the frameset. Authors introduce a technique for similarity matching of document framesets based on these maximal grid representations. The major bottleneck of this approach is choosing the fixed grid size, which leads to less flexibility. Also, this technique is sensitive to actual physical position of the blocks. For example, placement of a section title at a different position would affect the similarity measure, even though the relative arrangements of blocks in the document remains unchanged. On similar lines, authors in [7] present a two step method for layout comparison. They use different methods to compute the distance between image rows after doing segmentation into a grid of equal-sized cells. Each cell is identified as text cell if at least half of the cell is part of some text block, otherwise the cell is considered as a white space cell. Document images are then compared using dynamic programming on the row-based representation of the documents.

To overcome the issues of fixed grid size, hierarchical representation of the page layout, in the form of XY trees [3, 10] was proposed. In this approach similarity in terms of tree representation of documents is considered. The XY trees can exhibit high variability in their representation. To overcome the variability, the authors propose two approaches that rely on the use of tree-grammar based transformations of the XY trees. The first approach is based on query expansion, in which, given one query page, transformations are applied to the query XY tree to simulate variations in the tree that might correspond to actual variations in document images. Documents in the dataset are afterwards ranked on the basis of the similarity with the whole set of trees obtained from the query one. The second approach takes into account a different grammar to reduce the complexity of trees by removing tree structures that usually carry less information. The similarity is computed by evaluating the distance between the reduced query tree and reduced trees in the database. The similarity metric used in this approach is tree edit distance.

Gordo and Valveny [6] present a method to represent and classify document layouts based on a graph representation of the regions, which is later flattened into a cyclic sequence, obtaining a vector representation of the document layout. Kumar and Doermann [9] present a method for retrieval of document images with chosen layout characteristics. Their method is based on statistics of patch code words over different regions of image. A set of wanted and unwanted image representatives in a large heterogeneous collection is taken and raw-image patches are extracted from the unlabeled images to learn a codebook. To model the spatial relationships between patches, the image is recursively partitioned horizontally and vertically, and a histogram of patch codewords is computed in each partition. Training and learning is carried out using random forest classifiers.

In the spatial database domain, a lot of work has been done for building indexes such as R-trees, as illustrated in [5], which are designed for efficiently indexing spatial geometries according to their locations. An R-tree groups nearby objects and represents them with their minimum bounding rectangle in the next higher level of the tree. Types of spatial relations such as: contains, overlaps, intersects, etc. quite naturally correspond to the arrangement of information in documents in hierarchies such as letters, words, paragraphs, or cells, columns, tables. Thus, this is an efficient way to capture document layouts. In [4], the authors use a feature space which is derived by taking probability distributions of the text elements namely: word height, character width, horizontal word spacing, line spacing and line indentation. Authors build a histogram for each of these five layout features. Each histogram is then smoothed using a standard kernel function. A dissimilarity measure based on KL divergence is used for each layout feature as the distance between the distributions for that feature. Beusekom [2] consider a document as a composition of overlapping blocks and propose three distance metrics for matching two documents segmented into blocks. The distance metrics are computed by formulating three problems: (i) Assignment Problem, where each block is matched at most once, and the aim of the matching step is to match query and reference layout blocks by minimising a total cost that is the sum of all matches between two blocks multiplied by their cost that is given by the corresponding block distance. (ii) Minimum Weight Edge Cover Problem, which is the same as assignment problem except that every block of layout 1 is connected to at least one block of layout 2 and vice versa. (ii) Earth Movers Distance/Transportation Problem, where, each block is matched partially to at least one other block. Instead of matching entire blocks, here blocks are divided into pixels that are assigned to other blocks.

To summarise, layout features have been researched extensively in the past to aid in document retrieval and analysis.

1.2   Our Contributions

We propose a novel feature called attributed paths to capture the layout of documents. Attributed paths offer a great flexibility in capturing aspects that are closer to the semantics represented in the layout of document elements. Retrieval of sublayouts can be effectively done using attributed paths. Attributed paths admit a similarity computation based on edit distance and is therefore computationally efficient compared to graph-based layout matching methods.

2   Attributed Paths

An attributed path is simply a sequence of layout relevant attributes. A document can be represented using a set of attributed paths capturing a heterogeous set of semantics.

Let d be a document and $\mathcal{S}$ be a set of semantics. Let $\mathcal{P}_d^{\mathcal{S}}$ denote the set of attributed paths belonging to a set of semantics $\mathcal{S}$ for document d. The layout similarity measure for given two documents d_1 and d_2 is defined as:

$$\text{match}(\mathcal{P}_{d_1}^{\mathcal{S}}, \mathcal{P}_{d_2}^{\mathcal{S}}) = \sum_{s \in \mathcal{S}} w_s \times \text{match}(\mathcal{P}_{d_1}^s, \mathcal{P}_{d_2}^s) \tag{1}$$

where w_s is a user supplied weight factor that specifies the relative importance of the matching of attributed paths corresponding to semantic s. The function $\text{match}(\mathcal{P}_{d_1}^s, \mathcal{P}_{d_2}^s)$ deals with matching the sets of attributed paths having semantic s in document d_1 and d_2. The matching can be done by considering or ignoring the spatial organization of attributed paths in the sets $\mathcal{P}_{d_1}^s$ and $\mathcal{P}_{d_2}^s$.

Considering the dependence of the paths on semantics of the documents being considered, the path extraction process must be aware and exploit those semantics. The path extraction process and the matching process is thus not portable across diverse document categories. Instead, it requires modifications to the path extraction and matching methods, depending on the semantics relevant to the document category. In our work we consider two document categories to demonstrate the use of attributed paths for layout similarity. The first category is architectural floor plans [14] and the second category is journals [1].

Architectural Floor Plans. The semantic that we adopt for modeling layout of architectural floor plans correspond to the shortest valid navigational path from entry point of the floor to the exit point of the floor. In case the entry and the exit points coincide, or are too close, the navigational path is considered from the entry point to the center of the room farthest from the entrance. We call such navigational paths that begin at the entry point of the floor plan as the *principal paths*. A floor plan having a single entry and exit point will have a single principal path. Floor plans having multiple entries and exits will have multiple principal paths corresponding to separate entry-exit pairs. The principal path is the shortest navigational path which can pass through corridors and rooms containing two doors or passages. The principal path may not pass through all the rooms in the floor plan, i.e., it may exclude some rooms. Therefore, we introduce another semantic which corresponds to extracting navigational paths that connect the centers of the excluded rooms to the nearest point on a principal path. These paths that connect room centers to the principal path are called as *secondary paths*. Figure 1 shows the examples of principal and secondary paths overlaid on a floor plan. It is to be noted that the navigational paths involve 90^0 turns and follow Manhattan layout. All principal paths identified in the floor plan share the same semantic group. The secondary paths that connect to the same principal path are assigned a common semantic group, but that is distinct from the semantic of the principal path they connect to. Also, secondary paths that connect to a second principal path (if it is there) are assigned to a another semantic group. Thus, in a floor plan, there can be different semantic groups for secondary paths but a single semantic group for all the principal paths.

If the floor plan has multiple principal paths, we adopt a simple way to order them, by identifying a reference point in the top left corner of the floor plan and visiting the entry points in the floor plan in a clockwise order. Secondary paths that belong to the same semantic group (and thus connect to the same principal path) are ordered by traversing the principal path from entry point to exit and numbering the secondary paths in the order they are connected to the principal path.

We consider the {direction, length} pair as a composite attribute and consider the attributed path represented as a sequence of tuples. Direction is quantized into 4 values: N, S, E, W. The length represents the distance traversed along the path in the same direction, up to the next turn. We then compute the string edit distance by defining the substitution, insertion and deletion costs. The cost is proportional to the dissimilarity in the direction and the difference in the length values. We assign a higher weight to the similarity computed for the principal paths.

Text Documents: Pages from Journals. Refering to Fig. 2, we use the white space margin and white space column separators to extract the attributed paths. We identify the text columns and traverse the white space margin/separator which is to the left of the text column. The white space margin/separator is traversed from top to bottom and the attributed path is characterized by noting the top left corners of the text blocks adjacent (towards the right) to the margin. The attribute to be noted can include the syntactic/semantic label of the block and the intervening distances between the successive blocks. We compute the distance as the vertical distance between the top left corners of the successive blocks. The attributed path is characterized as a string containing block labels and intervening distances. Larger values of distance indicate presence of larger blocks. In this work we consider the block label as 'text', 'image', or 'table'. These labels are assigned based on grayscale statistics of the blocks and presence of line separators. A document may have multiple text columns and therefore require a separate attributed path to model the layout of each column. See Fig. 3 for another example showing attributed paths on a page from journal PAMI. The text blocks in a column are identified using the run length smearing algorithm. For documents, the paths are linear sequences of labels and attributes such as length. Unlike the floor plans, the attributed path in documents did not make any navigational turns. Moreover, for the case of documents, the attributed paths we extract have the same semantic.

In case of architectural floor plans, the paths corresponded to navigation in the floor plan and therefore they could take turns. These navigational paths resemble 2D skeletons. In literature, match measures have been proposed for 2D skeletons [11,12,16]. However, because our skeletons had simple left and right turns, we consider the proposed string encoding of the attributed path to be effective and computationally efficient.

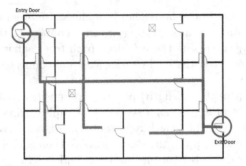

Fig. 1. A sample floor plan image. The red path is the principal path that connects the entry door to the exit door. The blue paths are the secondary paths that connect the centers of the rooms to the nearest point on the principal path. The encoding of the principal path is as follows: {(E, 104), (S, 230), (E, 285), (S, 42), (E, 84), (S, 39), (E, 186)}. (Color figure online)

Fig. 2. (a) Sample document from type a in MARG dataset (b) Segmented Layout and attributed path.

3   Experiments and Results

We demonstrate the performance of our feature set and matching procedure on two types of publicly available datasets: (1) ROBIN dataset [14] of architectural floor plans, (2) MARG (Medical Article Records Ground-truth) dataset [1].

Fig. 3. Sample document from PAMI dataset. Encoding for the attributed path for the left column is (T, 108), (Tb, 240), (T, 57), (T, 23), (T, 164) and for the right column is (T, 35), (T, 27), (T, 160), (I, 103), (T, 254).

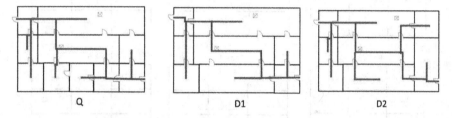

Fig. 4. The query image is shown to the left and the top two retrievals D1 and D2 from the dataset are shown. The attributed paths are overlaid on the images. The match costs for retrieved images D1 and D2 are 24 and 41, respectively. Image D2 has different number of rooms, and therefore a higher cost component contributed because of the secondary paths.

3.1   Results on ROBIN Dataset

ROBIN dataset contains 510 floor plan images divided into 3 broad categories of layouts, namely layouts with 3 rooms, 4 rooms and 5 rooms, respectively. There are 17 sub-categories differing in the global layout shape inside each category. Each sub-category further contains 10 layouts which have similar accessibility paths of each room from another room and varying placement of furniture. One such result between a query and two database images is illustrated in Fig. 4.

Retrieval results for another query from the floor plan dataset are shown in Fig. 5. Notice the similarity of the principal path for the top 5 retrieved results.

Figure 6 shows an example of a floor plan where there is a single entry but 3 exits. Therefore, there are 3 principal paths that lead from the entry to every exit. The top 5 matches show a similarity in terms of the principal paths. Figure 7 shows an example where the query floor plan happens to be a sublayout within the retrieved floor plan.

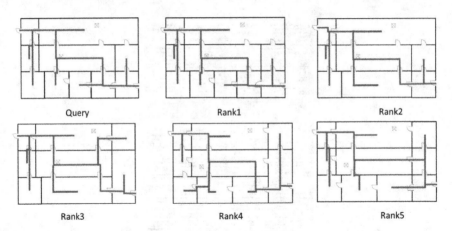

Fig. 5. Top 5 retrieved images for a floor plan query.

Fig. 6. Retrieval results for a floor plan with single entry and multiple exits

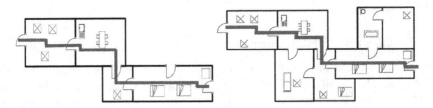

Fig. 7. Shows the retrieved result (right) for the query floor plan (left). The query layout can be considered as a sublayout within the retrieved result. The two floor plans have similar primary paths.

For quantifying our results on the ROBIN dataset we computed precision (P) values at every recall (R) value for all the 510 queries in the dataset while matching. The resultant PR curve obtained is shown in Fig. 8. The mean average precision value obtained on this dataset is 0.7997. As our approach of feature extraction and matching is aligned with skeletal path matching, therefore, for a fair comparison, we also implemented the technique of finding skeletal path using electoral voting for shape matching using features as proposed by authors in [8]. Under this approach nodes in skeletal paths between two documents were pruned based on a rule set and node correspondences were established. Further, the shape of the skeleton was aligned to another document skeleton using these equal node correspondences. Difference in alignment between two such skeletons was quantified through rotation and translation required to align one to another. As this technique involved pruning of the node set and not taking into consideration the whole path between two nodes, led to missing out on significant information while capturing the document layout for matching. Therefore, our approach of sampling the skeletal path and matching outperformed the technique mentioned in [8] by a significant margin. Our approach also outperforms the results obtained by our implementation of work reported in [13].

3.2   Results on MARG Dataset

MARG dataset [1] has been used for layout analysis tasks. It contains 815 scanned documents of first pages of medical journals, sorted by type (9 different types) and journal (161 different journals). We used this dataset for the purpose of document rerieval. We segmented the layouts of the documents in this dataset in terms of blocks and performed matching to depict which document is similar in terms of spatial arrangement of those blocks.

Queries to the MARG database can be of two categories (JOUR and TYPE), and therefore we report two types performance results.

– Journal (JOUR): There are document images from 161 different journals. For a given query we rank all the retrieved document. A retrieved document that belongs to the same journal is considered as a correct result. The quantitative analysis of our technique on the MARG dataset by categorizing the documents according to the journals gave us mean average precision value as 0.7780.
– Type (TYPE): This error rate gives the ratio of misclassifications of the document type. As there are only nine different layout types that need to be distinguished, thus it widens the number of documents in a particular type category, therefore, the retrieval performance is better. The mean average precision (MAP) value while categorizing the documents according to the Type yielded a MAP value of 0.950.

The PR curve for both the results is shown in Fig. 8, where the blue line corresponds to PR curve obtained by retrieval according to JOUR, and green line corresponds to retrieval according to TYPE in MARG dataset.

We now compare our scheme of attributed paths for layout matching with block-based layout matching proposed in Beusekom [2]. The comparative analysis yielded the results summarized in the Table 1. It can be observed that our matching technique is quite effective while retrieving documents belonging to

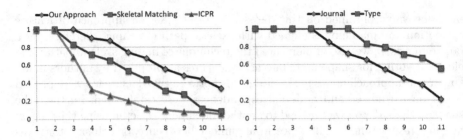

Fig. 8. (Left) PR plots obtained on ROBIN dataset for our approach, Skeletal path matching [8], and the approach published in ICPR [13]. (Right)PR plot obtained on MARG dataset, blue line corresponds to retrieval according to category Journal, green line corresponds to retrieval according to category Type (Color figure online)

the same journal on the MARG dataset. It improved the performance of classification by lowering the error rate by approximately 4%. However, the error rate obtained through categorizing into types was comparable to the Edge Cover distance measure and outperformed both Assignment and EMD distance measures.

Table 1. Error rate comparison with [2] on MARG dataset

Technique	Jour	Type
Edge cover	32.8	8.2
Assignment	52.0	22.9
EMD	52.3	20.2
Ours	**28.6**	**8.8**

To show the applicability of our algorithm on various other textual documents as well, we created a database of around 150 pages of papers published in PAMI in the year 2011. PAMI papers follow a certain uniform standard of layout representation, hence, are suitable for analysing our retrieval algorithm. We performed our feature extraction and matching on the documents and obtained encouraging results, as shown in Fig. 9. It is to be noted that the attributed paths were able to efficiently capture the placement of figures and the overall layout of the document while retrieving.

Use of attributed paths also makes it possible to do text column matching, instead of doing a full page layout matching. Since each column is represented as a separate attributed path, it is possible to match a 3-column document with a 2-column document. For this purpose, we took 25 3-column pages from IEEE control journal and matched those 3-column documents among themselves as well as with 2-column PAMI dataset documents. We got encouraging results. An example is shown in Fig. 10.

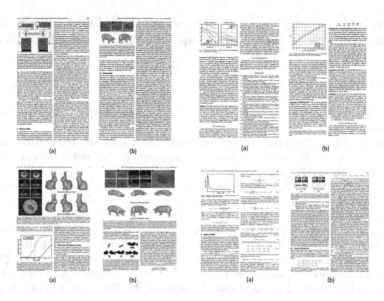

Fig. 9. Retrieval result on PAMI dataset using 4 query images. (a) Query document (b) Top retrieved document

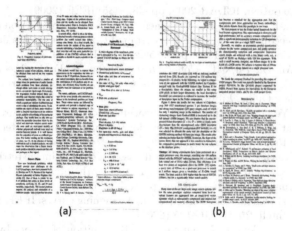

Fig. 10. Qualitative results obtained upon posing 3 column documents as query. (a) Query document (b) Retrieved document

4   Conclusions

We have proposed a novel feature called attributed paths to capture the layout of documents. Attributed paths offer a great flexibility in capturing aspects that are closer to the semantics represented in the layout of document elements. Our retrieval results on floor plans and journal documents are very encouraging. Retrieval of sublayouts can be effectively done using attributed paths. Attributed paths admit a similarity computation based on edit distance and is therefore computationally efficient compared to graph-based layout matching methods.

References

1. The Medical Article Records Groundtruth dataset. http://marg.nlm.nih.gov/roverintro.asp
2. Beusekom, J.V.: Diploma thesis: Document layout analysis. Image Understanding and Pattern Recognition Group, Department of Computer Science, Month Unknown, pp. 1–67 (2006)
3. Cesarini, F., Lastri, M., Marinai, S., Soda, G.: Encoding of modified XY trees for document classification. In: Proceedings of the Sixth International Conference on Document Analysis and Recognition, pp. 1131–1136. IEEE (2001)
4. Collins-Thompson, K., Nickolov, R.: A clustering-based algorithm for automatic document separation. In: SIGIR 2002 Workshop on Information Retrieval and OCR: From Converting Content to Grasping, Meaning, Tampere, Finland (2002)
5. Gao, H., Rusinol, M., Karatzas, D., Lladós, J.: Fast structural matching for document image retrieval through spatial databases. In: DRR, pp. 90,210N–90,210N (2014)
6. Gordo, A., Valveny, E.: A rotation invariant page layout descriptor for document classification and retrieval. In: 10th International Conference on Document Analysis and Recognition, ICDAR 2009, pp. 481–485. IEEE (2009)
7. Hu, J., Kashi, R., Wilfong, G.: Document image layout comparison and classification. In: Proceedings of the Fifth International Conference on Document Analysis and Recognition, ICDAR 1999, pp. 285–288. IEEE (1999)
8. Kin-Chung Au, O., Tai, C.L., Cohen-Or, D., Zheng, Y., Fu, H.: Electors voting for fast automatic shape correspondence. In: Computer Graphics Forum, vol. 29, pp. 645–654. Wiley Online Library (2010)
9. Kumar, J., Ye, P., Doermann, D.: Learning document structure for retrieval and classification. In: 2012 21st International Conference on Pattern Recognition (ICPR), pp. 1558–1561. IEEE (2012)
10. Marinai, S., Marino, E., Soda, G.: Layout based document image retrieval by means of XY tree reduction. In: Proceedings of the Eighth International Conference on Document Analysis and Recognition, pp. 432–436. IEEE (2005)
11. Sebastian, T.B., Klein, P.N., Kimia, B.B.: On aligning curves. IEEE Trans. Pattern Anal. Mach. Intell. **25**(1), 116–125 (2003)
12. Sebastian, T.B., Klein, P.N., Kimia, B.B.: Recognition of shapes by editing their shock graphs. IEEE Trans. Pattern Anal. Mach. Intell. **26**(5), 550–571 (2004)
13. Sharma, D., Chattopadhyay, C., Harit, G.: A unified framework for semnatic matching of architectural floorplans. In: ICPR (2016)
14. Sharma, D., Gupta, N., Chattopadhyay, C., Mehta, S.: DANIEL: a deep architecture for automatic analysis and retrieval of building floor plans. In: ICDAR (2017)
15. Tzacheva, A., El-Sonbaty, Y., El-Kwae, E.A.: Document image matching using a maximal grid approach. In: Proceedings of the SPIE, vol. 4670, p. 122 (2002)
16. Zhu, S.C., Yuille, A.L.: FORMS: a flexible object recognition and modelling system. Int. J. Comput. Vis. **20**(3), 187–212 (1996)

Textual Content Retrieval from Filled-in Form Images

Soulib Ghosh[1], Rajdeep Bhattacharya[1(✉)], Sandipan Majhi[1],
Showmik Bhowmik[1], Samir Malakar[2], and Ram Sarkar[1]

[1] Department of Computer Science and Engineering, Jadavpur University,
Kolkata, India
`ghoshsoulib@gmail.com`, `rajdeep.cse17@gmail.com`,
`sandipan.majhi.email@gmail.com`, `showmik.
cse@gmail.com`, `raamsarkar@gmail.com`
[2] Department of Computer Science, Asutosh College, Kolkata, India
`malakarsamir@gmail.com`

Abstract. Form processing refers to the process of extraction of information from filled-in forms. In this work, we have addressed three very crucial challenges of a form processing system, namely touching component separation, text non-text separation and handwritten-printed text separation. The proposed method is evaluated on a database having 50 filled-in forms written in Bangla, collected during an essay competition in a school. The experimental results are promising.

Keywords: Form processing · Text non-text separation ·
Handwritten-printed text separation · Touching component separation ·
Bangla text

1 Introduction

Form processing refers to the process of extracting the textual information present in a filled-in form. Forms have been preferred for information collection in various departments such as railway, bank, educational organization, administrative office, etc. Forms can be divided into various categories such as orders, applications, claims and survey forms. Huge volume of such forms generated in every department makes manual processing tedious. Thus, development of an automated form processing system becomes a pressing need.

Processing of filled-in forms, however, has many challenges such as the diversity that exists in the type of the data (e.g. numerals, alphabet, etc.), occurrence of various non-text elements (e.g. tables, lines of different types, logs, etc.) and presence of both printed and handwritten text. In addition to these, two more critical problems are there, one of which appears at the text extraction level which is occurrence of touching components, and the other appears at the text recognition level due to the complexity of handwritten text. In this work, a system is developed for the extraction of text present in a filled-in form, where we have addressed three major issues namely, touching component separation, text non-text separation, and handwritten-printed text separation.

© Springer Nature Singapore Pte Ltd. 2019
S. Sundaram and G. Harit (Eds.): DAR 2018, CCIS 1020, pp. 27–37, 2019.
https://doi.org/10.1007/978-981-13-9361-7_3

2 Related Work

Methods used for text non-text separation in filled-in form images are broadly classified into three groups – region based, connected component (CC) based and pixel based classification. In region based classification, the entire image is divided into regions and then each region is identified as a text or non-text region. In this category, mostly texture based features are used such as white tiles based features [1], run length based features [2], gray level co-occurrence matrix (GLCM) based features [3], etc. However, region based classification falters in cases where textual regions are highly scattered which become very challenging during segmentation. In CC level classification, each component is identified as text or non-text. In [4], Bhowmik et al. have applied Rotation Invariant Local Binary Pattern (RILBP) based features to characterize the component as text or non-text. In [5], Le et al. have studied shapes and sizes of CCs to extract effective set of features based on size, shape, stroke width and position to characterize each CC. Though component level classification provides good results in general, it fails in case of documents where components overlap each other due to poor binarization. To overcome these limitations, recently researchers have proposed pixel based classification [6] to classify each pixel as text or non-text pixel. But the main drawback of pixel based classification is its time consumption. A detailed study of text non-text separation in document image can be found in the survey paper by Bhowmik et al. [7]. In [8, 9], researchers have proposed line and table detection methods from document images. These methods require preprocessing steps and fail to provide good results for complex cases where lines or tables are not exactly vertical/horizontal.

In [10], Pal et al. have described machine-printed and handwritten text classification scheme based on statistical features for Bangla and Devanagari scripts. Chanda et al. [11] have proposed a method for separating handwritten and printed text in the perspective of sparse data and random alignment. They have used Support Vector Machine (SVM) classifier and chain-code feature vector for this purpose. The work presented in [12] consists of patch level separation and pixel level separation. Three different classes - machine printed text, handwritten text and overlapped text are initially identified using G-means (modified version of K-means) based classification followed by an MRF based relabeling procedure. In [13], Malakar et al. have extracted a 6-element feature set from each image first and then a decision tree classifier has been designed to perform the classification.

The most accurate methods are time consuming whereas the faster methods fail to provide good results in the presence of critical challenges. Textual regions in document forms are distributed throughout the entire image due to the handwritten text fields. Thus, the approach of isolating polygonal regions for textual parts will not serve the purpose due to which we avoid typical region based classification. Further pixel level classification is time consuming and hence, we restrict our method to component level classification.

3   Proposed Work

Entire work presented here has some key modules which are shown in Fig. 1.

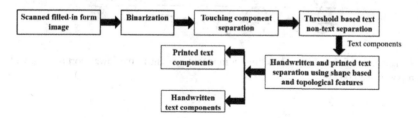

Fig. 1. Flowchart of the proposed filled-in form processing method showing all the key modules.

3.1   Detection and Separation of Touching Components

Touching text/non-text components are very common in filled-in forms (see Fig. 2) and hence detection and thereby separation of touching components is a pressing need. A method is proposed here for the said purpose which consists of two steps. The components touching the substantially large horizontal lines, mainly occurring as parts of tables, are detected in the first step and then detached in the second step.

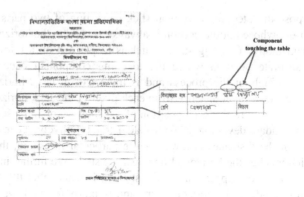

Fig. 2. Examples of touching components in a table.

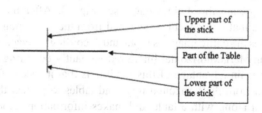

Fig. 3. Orientation of the stick on a line. The middle of the stick is attached to the line.

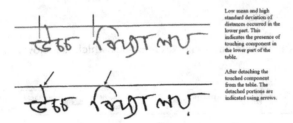

Low mean and high
standard deviation of
distances occurred in the
lower part. This
indicates the presence of
touching component in
the lower part of the
table.

After detaching the
touched component
from the table. The
detached portions are
indicated using arrows.

Fig. 4. Example of detaching a touching component present in the lower portion of a table by the proposed method.

বিদ্যালয়ের নাম	ত্রাউতাপ্রপস্যার ঐচ্চ, বিগ্রানেন	
শ্রেণি	বেশগাদিতা	বিভাগ

(a)

বিদ্যালয়ের নাম	ত্রাউতাপ্রপস্যার ঐচ্চ, বিগ্রানেন	
শ্রেণি	বেশগাদিতা	বিভাগ

(b)

Fig. 5. Text non-text classification results. Denotes the classification result: (a) before applying our method, (b) after applying our method. Red denotes text and green color denotes tables. Only the zoomed portion is shown for clarity. The modified portions are indicated using arrows. (Color figure online)

For the purpose of detection, a vertical stick consisting of two parts – upper and lower, is introduced whose middle portion is always clinched to the horizontal line (see Fig. 3). The main motive of using such a stick is to place it on a horizontal line to determine the accurate position where the touching component occurs. The stick remains vertical throughout the process and is traversed on large horizontal line to calculate the nearest data pixel distance from each pixel of the stick horizontally in the forward direction. Therefore, for each position of the stick we obtain a set of distances whose mean and standard deviation (SD) are calculated. Intuitively, it can be concluded that if the mean of the distances is lower than a particular threshold, then there is a component which touches the horizontal line near the stick. We further infer that if the low distances occur on the upper part of the stick, it indicates that the component is hooked on the upper side of the horizontal line and similarly for the lower part as well. SD is additionally used to check for the cursive nature of the touching component. The proper presence of any touching component can be assured if mean is less and SD is more than the appropriate threshold values (see Fig. 4). After the detection of the touching component, that component is detached from the horizontal line (see Fig. 4).

This method takes the entire image as input and accordingly detaches all the touching components from any large horizontal line, predominantly occurring in the horizontal part of a table. The main advantage of this module is that it successfully detaches the touching component from the horizontal lines and tables to protect them from getting classified as non-text along with a table and makes information retrieval more appropriate (see Fig. 5). This, in turn, makes the text non-text classification less complex.

3.2 Text Non-text Separation

In this module, we aim to separate the text components from the non-text components. We have identified an exhaustive list of non-text components that may occur in a form and handled each of those separately. First, we have extracted all the CCs from an image and excluded the components whose area is very small (say less than α_1). It is found that such components usually represent stray marks and hence are ignorable. Then for the components with area more than the said threshold value, we have performed the following operations.

Line Separation: For text, the lines usually appear as 'Matra' or strikethrough which occur in conjunction with a word as one single CC and, hence, are handled along with them. Here, we deal with standalone lines, which are generally used to separate one part of the document from another or act as a base for the user to write on. For separating these lines, we use the following feature.

$$\frac{\max\{height, width\}}{\min\{height, width\}} \tag{1}$$

We note that in case of a line, either the width is very large compared to the height (in case of horizontal line) or the height is very large compared to its width. We classify it as a line, and hence non-text, if this ratio is greater than a certain threshold value (say β_1) in either case.

Table Separation: We note that a table would cover a significant portion of the area of the form and at least one out of the height and width will be of large magnitude. Hence, according to our algorithm, a component is said to be a table if it satisfies the following condition.

$$\text{(component height} > \gamma_1 \times \text{height of the image)} \\ \text{or (component width} > \gamma_2 \times \text{height of the image)} \tag{2}$$

Here, $0 \le \gamma_1 < 1$ and $0 \le \gamma_2 < 1$
Here, the values of γ_1 and γ_2 are chosen experimentally.

Dot Separation: In this section, we begin by checking if the area of the component is in a certain range that most dots satisfy. If so, we check if both the height and width are greater than a certain number of pixels (say $\in$), which is chosen to be sufficiently large, as otherwise, even a small line might satisfy the area threshold. If it satisfies the above conditions, then the component can be classified as a dot. Now, a dot can be text or non-text. For example, in Fig. 6, the Bangla letter contains a dot as descender. For this, we have considered the context information of an identified dot. We have measured the average CC height σ after table and line separation, and scanned σ number of pixels above and below the dot. If we find sufficient number of data pixels (greater than a certain threshold τ), it is classified as a text dot, otherwise non-text dot.

Fig. 6. (a) Dot as a part of text (b) scanning of upper region for context information.

Strikethrough Separation: If the component is not small enough to be a dot as well, then we check for strikethrough. The feature used for this is mainly Euler number as we note that for a skeleton of a strikethrough, the Euler number becomes low. For this, we first swell the component up so that any negligible gap in the handwriting is filled up. The parameters for swell are so given that only the ink gaps which are left in the course of writing are filled and not the larger ones. Then we take the morphological skeleton of the component. We note that for a strikethrough on a word or character, it intersects the same at quite a few points and hence these intersections create many holes. This decreases the Euler number significantly for the strikethrough components. An example is provided in Fig. 7 for reference.

Fig. 7. A strikethrough component and its skeleton after it is swelled up.

As it can be understood from the image, the Euler number of the second component is less as the number of holes in it is very high. Thus, we set a threshold (say, α_2) where if the Euler number of this skeleton is less than α_2, then the component is classified as strikethrough and hence non-text, else text.

Bracket Separation: If the component satisfies none of the above checks, then we examine whether it is a bracket or not. We again swell up the component and take the morphological skeleton of it. This step reduces the stroke width significantly and ensures that the thickness of the bracket is not an issue for further processing. Then we analyze the component row-wise. If in any row, we find that the number of data pixels crosses a certain threshold (say β_2), then we classify it as a non-bracket, else bracket. This is illustrated in Fig. 8.

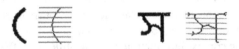

Fig. 8. Demonstration of row-wise scanning of a skeletonized bracket and non-bracket component. Here, for the bracket, no row encounters a significant number of data pixels. This is because a bracket is generally written in a single stroke as shown.

3.3 Handwritten and Printed Text Separation

In this module of our work, an effort has been made to successfully segregate the handwritten and printed text present in the form images. For this, following features are extracted from the components.

Otsu Threshold: Printed text has a fixed typeset and uniform pixel intensity, so Otsu threshold is supposed to be almost similar for all of them, and these values for all printed text should converge to a fixed value. The same is not true for handwritten text because of non-uniformity in ink flow, hand pressure etc.

SD of Pixel Intensities: The gray scale image of a CC of printed text is assumed to be having mostly similar pixel intensity which is not true for handwritten text. Hence, SD of the pixel intensities of printed text becomes less than the SD of handwritten text.

Entropy: Entropy is a statistical measure which is viewed as the amount of information available in a data distribution. Handwritten text contains more variations in gray level values than printed text and hence possess less entropy value. It is so because printed text attains almost same pixel intensity patterns of the source, which is the typeset of the document processor. Entropy (H) of a gray scale image can be computed from its histogram counts p_n by the Eq. (3).

$$H = -\sum_{n=0}^{255} p_n \log_2 p_n \qquad (3)$$

Stroke Width: As the format of printed text are set beforehand in a document processor, the stroke width remains fairly fixed with respect to the set value. However, this is not true for handwritten text. Hence, stroke width is considered in four different directions for the said analysis. The four directions that are considered are horizontal, vertical, left diagonal and right diagonal (see Fig. 9). In this context, the mean and SD of the stroke widths of all directions are taken.

Fig. 9. Determination of stroke width along four directions. The red lines correspond to the continuity in pixels along a particular direction. (Color figure online)

Distribution of Contour to Boundary Pixel Maps: Some variations in the curvatures and orientations of the strokes are found while writing same symbol (see Fig. 10). Therefore, in order to include these variations, the said features are considered. From each pixel in the contour of a CC, the minimum distance from each of the boundaries of the component is measured. The closest boundary from a particular pixel gets a contribution of 1 while other get a contribution of 0. In this way, the pixels are distributed among the four boundaries (see Fig. 11). At last, the SDs of these distributions along each boundary are taken as features.

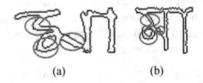

(a)   (b)

Fig. 10. Same word written in (a) handwritten form. (b) printed form. Red circular regions denote the differences in shapes and curvature, between (a) & (b) in similar regions. (Color figure online)

4 Experimental Results

As there is no publicly available dataset related to filled-in form in *Bangla* script, hence a dataset is prepared for the evaluation of the proposed method which consists of 50 forms. A sample form image taken from our database is shown in Fig. 12a and the corresponding ground truth (GT) image is shown in Fig. 12b. The GT for each scanned form is created manually. To assess the performance of text non-text separation module, the final outputs after applying our methods are evaluated with the previously produced GTs. For evaluating handwritten-printed text classification, CCs from the last 30 forms are considered to train a *Random Forest* classifier, whereas the CCs of the first 20 forms are used for testing. A total of 42,324 CCs are present in these collected forms, out of which non-text, printed and handwritten CCs are 4784, 18437 and 19103 in number respectively.

After exhaustive experimentation over a variety of data, the following thresholds have been set optimally: $\alpha_1 = 6$, $\beta_1 = 50$, $\gamma_1 = 0.16$, $\gamma_2 = 0.4$, $\in = 7$, $\sigma = 40$, $\tau = 3$, $\alpha_2 = -9$ and $\beta_2 = 5$. Also, the range of area referred to in dot separation is 50 to 100.

To evaluate the proposed method, we have considered three popular metrics *Precision, Recall* and *Accuracy* [7]. Detailed results for each of these modules are described in Table 1. From this table, it can be observed that our proposed method performs satisfactorily. It is to be noted that all these measurements are done at CC level. A sample image and its corresponding text non-text separated and handwritten-printed text separated images are shown in Fig. 13.

Also, some of the erroneous results are shown in Fig. 14. The touching component module fails when a text component touches a vertical line of any table. Text non-text separation module falters in the situation of a text overlapping with a stamp which causes a sufficient decrease of Euler number and results in the component being misclassified as a strikethrough. In case of very less cursive and non-complex handwritten text, it is also misclassified as printed text.

Fig. 11. The intersection point of the four colored lines denote the concerned pixel. Red, green, blue and yellow lines denote the distances of that pixel from the top, right, bottom, and left boundaries respectively. As it can be seen, the blue line is of smallest length and hence the contribution of that point for the bottom boundary is counted as 1 and for the rest as 0. (Color figure online)

Fig. 12. (a) Sample image taken from our dataset, (b) corresponding GT. Here red represents printed text, blue represents handwritten text, green represents non-text, yellow represents printed numerals and gray represents handwritten numerals. (Color figure online)

Table 1. Detailed experimental outcomes obtained by the different modules of the proposed method

Module	Precision	Recall	Accuracy
Text/Non-text separation	92.37%	90.47%	86.03%
Text/Non-text separation + Touching separation	93.27%	91.55%	87.65%
Handwritten-printed separation	95.8%	98.7%	96.2%

Fig. 13. Example of final output obtained by our proposed method. (a) sample input image, (b) corresponding text non-text separated image (c) corresponding handwritten-printed text separated image. Green color denotes non-text. Red color denotes text part in text non-text separated image and printed text in the final output whereas blue color denotes handwritten text in the final output. (Color figure online)

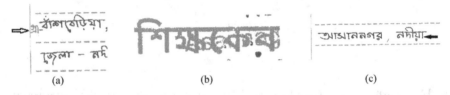

Fig. 14. Examples of several errors encountered while using our proposed method. Error encountered in (a) Touching component separation (b) Text non-text separation (c) Handwritten-printed separation module. Green color denotes non-text. In (c), Red color denotes printed component and Blue color denotes handwritten component. (Color figure online)

5   Conclusion

In this paper, we propose a text extraction technique from filled-in form images written in *Bangla* script. It comprises a novel touching component elimination method and a hybrid approach to decide trade-off between threshold and machine learning based approaches. Along with that some useful shape based and topological features are used for the separation of handwritten-printed text separation. All the used features are calculated without using any language heuristic. Hence, the method can also be applied to filled-in forms written in other languages. We plan to make use of dynamic values of certain parameters in the next scope of our work. The method for eliminating touching components can also be modified further to handle both horizontally and vertically touched components.

Acknowledgement. S. Bhowmik is thankful to Ministry of Electronics and Information Technology, Govt. of India, for providing PhD-Fellowship under Visvesvaraya PhD scheme.

References

1. Antonacopoulos, A., Ritchings, T.R., De Tran, C.: Representation and classification of complex-shaped printed regions using white tiles. In Proceedings of the Third International Conference on Document Analysis and Recognition, Montreal, QC, Canada, 14–16 August 1995, vol. 2, pp. 1132–1135 (1995)
2. Park, H.C., Ok, S.Y., Cho, H.: Word extraction in text/graphic mixed image using 3-dimensional graph model. In: Proceedings of the ICCPOL, Tokushima, Japan, 24–26 March 1999, vol. 99, pp. 171–176 (1999)
3. Oyedotun, O.K., Khashman, A.: Document segmentation using textural features summarization and feedforward neural network. Appl. Intell. **45**, 198–212 (2016)
4. Bhowmik, S., Sarkar, R., Nasipuri, M.: Text and non-text separation in handwritten document images using local binary pattern operator. In: Mandal, J., Satapathy, S., Sanyal, M., Bhateja, V. (eds.) International Conference on Intelligent Computing and Communication, pp. 507–515. Springer, Singapore (2017). https://doi.org/10.1007/978-981-10-2035-3_52
5. Le, V.P., Nayef, N., Visani, M., Ogier, J.-M., De Tran, C.: Text and non-text segmentation based on connected component features. In: Proceedings of the 2015 13th International Conference on Document Analysis and Recognition (ICDAR), Tunis, Tunisia, 23–26 August 2015, vol. 45, pp. 1096–1100 (2015)
6. Garz, A., Sablatnig, R., Diem, M.: Layout analysis for historical manuscripts using sift features Document. In: Proceedings of the 2011 International Conference on Document Analysis and Recognition (ICDAR), Beijing, China, 18–21 September 2011 (2011)
7. Bhowmik, S., Sarkar, R., Nasipuri, M., Doermann, D.: Text and non-text separation in offline document images: a survey. Int. J. Doc. Anal. Recognit. (IJDAR) **21**(1–2), 1–20 (2018)
8. Gatos, B., Danatsas, D., Pratikakis, I., Perantonis, S.J.: Automatic table detection in document images. In: Singh, S., Singh, M., Apte, C., Perner, P. (eds.) ICAPR 2005. LNCS, vol. 3686, pp. 609–618. Springer, Heidelberg (2005). https://doi.org/10.1007/11551188_67
9. Arvind, K.R., Kumar, J., Ramakrishnan, A.G.: Line removal and restoration of handwritten strokes. In: International Conference on Computational Intelligence and Multimedia Applications (ICCIMA 2007), Sivakasi, Tamil Nadu, India. IEEE (2007)
10. Pal, U., Chaudhuri, B.B.: Machine-printed and handwritten text lines identification. Pattern Recogn. Lett. **22**(3–4), 431–441 (2001)
11. Chanda, S., Franke, K., Pal, U.: Structural handwritten and machine print classification for sparse content and arbitrary oriented document fragments. In: Conference: Proceedings of the 2010 ACM Symposium on Applied Computing (SAC), Switzerland, 22–26 March 2010 (2010)
12. Peng, X., Setlur, A., Govindaraju, V., Sitaram, R.: Handwritten text separation from annotated machine printed documents using Markov random fields. Int. J. Doc. Anal. Recogn. (IJDAR) **16**(1), 1–16 (2013)
13. Malakar, S., Das, R.K., Sarkar, R., Basu, S., Nasipuri, M.: Handwritten and printed word identification using gray-scale feature vector and decision tree classifier. Procedia Technol. **10**, 831–839 (2013)

Handwriting Recognition and Symbol Spotting

A Study on the Effect of CNN-Based Transfer Learning on Handwritten Indic and Mixed Numeral Recognition

Rahul Pramanik$^{(\boxtimes)}$, Prabhat Dansena, and Soumen Bag

Department of Computer Science and Engineering,
Indian Institute of Technology (ISM) Dhanbad, Dhanbad, India
rahul.wbsu@gmail.com, p.dansena23@gmail.com, soumen@iitism.ac.in

Abstract. Filling up forms at post offices, railway counters, and for application of jobs has become a routine for modern people, especially in a developing country like India. Research on automation for the recognition of such handwritten forms has become mandatory. This applies more for a multilingual country like India. In the present work, we use readily available pre-trained Convolutional Neural Network (CNN) architectures on four different Indic scripts, viz. Bangla, Devanagari, Oriya, and Telugu to achieve a satisfactory recognition rate for handwritten Indic numerals. Furthermore, we have mixed Bangla and Oriya numerals and applied transfer learning for recognition. The main objective of this study is to realize how good a CNN model trained on an entire different dataset (of natural images) works for small and unrelated datasets. As a part of practical application, we have applied the proposed approach to recognize Bangla handwritten pin codes after their extraction from postal letters.

Keywords: Alexnet · CNN · Handwritten numerals · Transfer learning · VGG-16

1 Introduction

The widespread use of computers in our daily lives demand more digital and automated involvement. As such, the day to day entry in hard-bound registers at government institute and offices, filling of forms in banks, and sorting of handwritten letters at post offices needs to be automated for faster and efficient processing. However, in order to perfect such automation procedure, research and development needs to be carried out at a large scale for handwritten text recognition. Handwritten numeral recognition is a sub part of handwritten text recognition and involves classification and recognition of handwritten digits of 10 classes from 0 to 9. Although, extensive experimentation for the recognition of handwritten numerals have been carried out in the past decade on Arabic [1,2], Chinese [3], and English [4–6] scripts, but the same amount of work have not

© Springer Nature Singapore Pte Ltd. 2019
S. Sundaram and G. Harit (Eds.): DAR 2018, CCIS 1020, pp. 41–51, 2019.
https://doi.org/10.1007/978-981-13-9361-7_4

reflected for Indic scripts. The circumstance that makes handwritten numeral recognition for Indic scripts more challenging is the presence of implicit disparity in writing styles of various individuals.

The constitution of India recognises 23 different languages based on 12 scripts [7]. The recognised languages are Assamese, Bangla, Bodo, Dogri, English, Gujarati, Hindi, Kannada, Kashmiri, Konkani, Punjabi, Maithili, Malayalam, Manipuri, Marathi, Nepali, Oriya, Sanskrit, Santhali, Sindhi, Tamil, Telugu, and Urdu. The corresponding scripts for writing these languages are Bangla, Devanagari, Gujarati, Gurumukhi, Kannada, Malayalam, Manipuri, Oriya, Roman, Tamil, Telugu, and Urdu [8]. Over 1.4 billion people speak the aforementioned languages. It is a common situation in India where the different forms need to be filled by hand in government and public institutions like railway ticket counters, banks, post offices, etc. are filled using different scripts by people coming from different geographical background. The methodologies developed for handwritten text recognition generally do not incorporate the recognition of digits. This is because the features required for the text recognition may not be applicable for identifying the digits. As such, in a multilingual country like India, the need of an automated system for handwritten numeral recognition is severe.

1.1 Related Works

Most works that have been investigated till now is based on defining different feature set with combination of various classifiers for a particular Indic script. Khan et al. [9] have utilised Sparse Representation Classifier on image zone density for classification of Bangla numerals. Hassan and Khan [10] have applied three different variations of Linear Binary Pattern (LBP) in combination with K-NN classifier for recognising Bangla numerals. Sarkhel et al. [11] have used Non-Dominated Sorting Harmony-Search Algorithm (NSHA) and Non-Dominated Sorting Genetic Algorithm-II (NSGA-II) for selecting local regions and extracted certain structural features. They employed SVM classifier for identification of Bangla numerals. Singh et al. [12] have selected features based on maximum relevance minimum redundancy and conditional mutual information maximization and utilised MLP classifier for recognition of handwritten Devanagari numerals. Prabhanjan and Dinesh [13] have extracted pixel density statistics and Fourier Descriptors from handwritten Devanagari numerals for creating the feature set. They fused four different classifiers using stacking for final recognition. Similarly, Roy et al. [14] have used chain code histogram for feature extraction and Neural Network (NN) classifier and quadratic classifier for identification of handwritten Oriya numerals. Bhowmik et al. [15] have delineated a HMM based recognition approach where the states of the HMM are automatically determined based on handwritten Oriya digit images.

Apart from the aforementioned conventional approaches, recent research works are focussing more on utilising CNN for recognition of handwritten numerals. Shopon et al. [16] have used pre-trained auto encoder along with CNN for recognition of handwritten Bangla digits. Alom et al. [17] have delineated a set of 2 convolutional layer based CNN for handwritten Bangla numeral recognition. But, there exist only a handful of work that have tried to provide solution towards script independent handwritten numeral recognition. Bhattacharya and Chaudhuri [18] have illustrated a multi stage recognition strategy utilising wavelet based representations and MLP for Bangla, Devanagari, and English handwritten numerals. Singh *et al.* [19] have utilised a 130 dimensional feature set comprising of six different moments, viz. affine moment invariant, complex moment, geometric moment, Legendre moment, moment invariant, and Zernike moment along with MLP classifier for classification of Arabic, Bangla, Devanagari, English, and Telugu handwritten numerals. Maitra *et al.* [20] have used a LeNet-5 type CNN architecture for recognising Bangla, Devanagari, English, Oriya, and Telugu handwritten numerals.

1.2 Motivation

From the literature, we realised that defining a proper set of hand crafted features that may work across scripts is very difficult and may not work well across all scripts. Combining that chosen feature set with proper classifier is another difficult task. As such, recent research has focussed towards CNN based approaches. But, CNNs have two substantial restrictions. First, CNNs built from scratch requires a large amount of data for proper training. And, second, CNNs when trained from scratch requires a substantial amount of resource and time for training. Keeping the aforementioned difficulties under consideration, we provide the following solutions:

– Utilising readily available pre-trained CNN architectures on four different Indic scripts, viz. Bangla, Devanagari, Oriya, and Telugu to achieve a satisfactory recognition rate;
– It is not feasible to mix numerals of two Indic scripts due to the presence of same shape and structure to represent different numbers of one or more numerals in these scripts, which may result in higher misclassification error. Keeping this limitation in mind, we have mixed Bangla and Oriya script numerals, as both share only zero digit with same structure and applied transfer learning for recognition.
– As a part of practical application, we have applied the aforementioned approach to recognize Bangla handwritten pin codes after their extraction from postal letters.

The rest of the paper is systematized as follows: Sect. 2 delineates the current approach; Sect. 3 shows the results found and their analysis; Finally, Sect. 4 concludes the paper.

2 Proposed Method

Statistically, we can express a domain $\mathcal{D}$ through a feature space χ and a marginal probability distribution P(X), where $X = x_1, ..., x_n \ \forall x_i \in \chi$ [21]. Since, our task is image classification, and say if edges of the images are taken as features, so, χ will be the space for all edge vectors, x_i will be the $i^t h$ edge vector, and X will be a particular learning sample. For a specific domain, $\mathcal{D} = \{\chi, \mathrm{P(X)}\}$, a task is comprised of a pair of components: a label space Y and an objective predictive function f$(\cdot)$ (denoted by $\mathrm{T} = \{\mathrm{Y}, \mathrm{f}(\cdot)\}$). f$(\cdot)$ is learned from the training data consisting of pairs $\{x_i, y_i\}$, where $x_i \in$ X and $y_i \in$ Y. After the completion of the training process, the predictive function f$(\cdot)$ is used to predict the label for a new instance x.

Transfer Learning, for a source domain $\mathcal{D}_S$ with a learning task $\mathcal{L}_S$ and a target domain $\mathcal{D}_T$ with a learning task $\mathcal{L}_T$, can be defined as the procedure of refining the learning of the target predictive function $f_T(\cdot)$ in $\mathcal{D}_T$ using the information from $\mathcal{D}_S$ and $\mathcal{L}_S$, where $\mathcal{D}_S \neq \mathcal{D}_T$ or $\mathcal{L}_S \neq \mathcal{L}_T$. $f_{ST}(\cdot)$ is denoted as the predictive model which is initially trained on $\mathcal{D}_S$ and domain-adapted to $\mathcal{D}_T$. For example, in image classification approach, between the source image set and the target image set, either the features are different between the two sets or their marginal distributions are different. In the present approach, the difference is in marginal distributions.

We investigate two different CNN architectures: AlexNet [22] and VGG-16 [23]. AlexNet topped the 2012 ImageNet challenge, making CNNs popular. Alexnet comprises of 5 convolutional and max-pooling layers followed by 3 fully connected layers encompassing local response normalization layers and drop outs. It operates on $227 \times 227 \times 3$ RGB images. VGG-16 comprises of a much denser architecture when compared with Alexnet. It contains 13 convolutional layers along with max-pooling and rectification layers, followed by 3 fully connected layers. Each convolutional layer in VGG-16 architecture use 3 $\times$ 3 filters and max-pooling is performed with only 2×2 filters. The receptive field of VGG-16 is of size 224×224. VGG-16 is denser than Alexnet, and correspondingly it has 3$\times$ more parameters requiring more computation. As the pre-trained Alexnet is designed for 227×227 images with 3 corresponding channels, all input numeral images are preprocessed ($\mathrm{I} \in \mathbb{R}^{227 \times 227}$) and the same plane is concatenated thrice ($\mathrm{I} \in \mathbb{R}^{3 \times 227 \times 227}$). Similarly, VGG-16 is designed for 224×224 images with 3 corresponding channels. So, for this architecture, all numeral images are preprocessed ($\mathrm{I} \in \mathbb{R}^{224 \times 224}$) and the same plane is concatenated thrice ($\mathrm{I} \in \mathbb{R}^{3 \times 224 \times 224}$). The final 3 layers of both the pre-trained architectures are designed for 1000 classes. For each of the pre-trained architectures, we copied all the layers from $\mathcal{D}_S$ to $\mathcal{D}_T$ except the last fully connected layer. We reconstructed the final fully connected layers in order to adapt the model to our numeral classification problem. We added a fully connected layer, a softmax layer, and a classification layer at the end of the model which are randomly initialised and trained from scratch (Fig. 1). We train both the architectures using the minibatch stochastic gradient descent with momentum. Both network architectures are trained for 60 epochs. We use a batch size of 20 images for AlexNet as well as VGG-16 due to memory constraints.

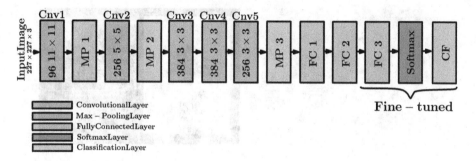

Fig. 1. Alexnet with illustration of transferred layers and fine-tuning.

2.1 Practical Application

As a practical application, we have applied transfer learning on extracted pin codes from post cards written in Bangla script. For extraction of the pin code, given a post card (Fig. 2a), we first binarize the image (Fig. 2b). This is followed by extraction of connected components. We remove the connected components whose width to height ratio is less than 4 (Fig. 2c). We have experimented with values between 1 and 10 and found 4 to be the most suitable one. Pin codes are generally written in a series of boxes specified in post cards. On the basis of this inference, we conclude that such a series of boxes will create the largest component among all the connected components. But, there can be other large components as well. In order to confirm that we identify the pin code boxed part only, we fill all the closed area with foreground pixels (Fig. 2d). Due to the presence of 6 connected boxes in the pin code area, after filling, a very large component gets created. We extract the largest component (Fig. 2e). Now, we perform bitwise AND operation between the currently generated figure (Fig. 2e) with the binarized image (Fig. 2b) to obtain the actual pin code area along with the numerals inside them (Fig. 2f). Next, we compute the bounding box of each of the boxes and extract the numerals as separate components, followed by removal of smaller components using a noise removal strategy [24] (Fig. 2g).

3 Experimental Results and Analysis

3.1 Datasets

We have used handwritten numeral images of 4 popular scripts, viz. Bangla, Devanagari, Oriya, and Telugu, for investigating the effectiveness of transfer learning. We have employed the ISI Oriya [25] numeral database for Oriya script. For Bangla, Devanagari, and Telugu scripts, we have employed CMATERdb dataset versions 3.1.1 [26,27], 3.2.1 [26,27], and 3.4.1 [26,27] respectively. A sample of few numeral images from each of these datasets is delineated in Table 1. To illustrate the efficiency of transfer learning, we have created a mixed script of Bangla and Oriya using the CMATERdb 3.1.1 dataset and ISI Oriya Numeral

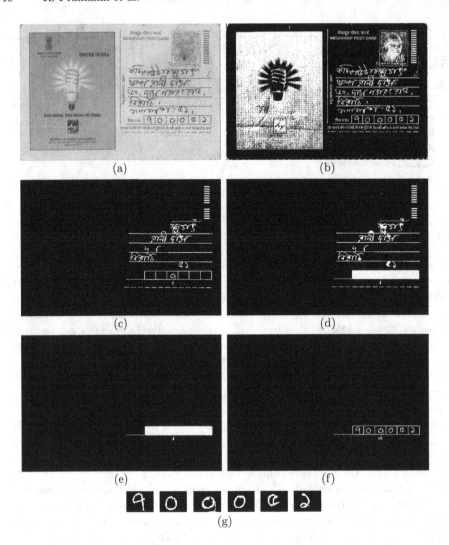

Fig. 2. Automated extraction of pin codes from post cards. (a) Input image; (b) After binarization; (c) After removal of connected components with width to height ratio ≤ 4; (d) Filling of connected components is performed; (e) Largest component is extracted; (f) Bitwise AND operation is performed with the binarized image; (g) Extraction of the pin codes as separate components.

dataset. Since the structure of zero is common for both the scripts, we created a training and testing set of 19 classes. A detailed overview of each of the datasets are provided in Table 2. For extraction and recognition of Bangla pin codes, we have used the CMATERdb 5.1 dataset [28]. The dataset consists of 50 post cards written in Bangla and English script. Among them, we have used the 28 post cards written in Bangla script for our current experimentation. The entire

Table 1. Few sample numeral images used in the current work for each of the script.

Script	Sample Images
Bangla	
Devanagari	
Oriya	
Telugu	

Table 2. Detailed overview of the datasets used.

Dataset	Script	Total # images	Train split	Test split	# Class
CMATERdb 3.1.1	Bangla	6000	4000	2000	10
CMATERdb 3.2.1	Devanagari	3000	2000	1000	
ISI Oriya	Oriya	5970	4970	1000	
CMATERdb 3.4.1	Telugu	3000	2000	1000	
CMATERdb 3.1.1 + ISI Oriya	Bangla + Oriya (Mixed)	11970	8970	3000	19

implementation and development of modules is carried out in Matlab. We used a 4GB Nvidia 940mx graphics card along with 8GB RAM Intel Core i5 processor to carry out the experiments.

3.2 Results and Analysis

This section delineates the experimental results of our current work. Here, we have provided a detailed analysis of the accuracies obtained by the proposed

Table 3. Accuracy achieved on different scripts.

Dataset	Script	Weight Updation	Accuracy (%) Alexnet	VGG-16
CMATERdb 3.1.1	Bangla	sgdm	95.00	93.33
CMATERdb 3.2.1	Devanagari		94.72	93.33
ISI Oriya	Oriya		94.50	93.00
CMATERdb 3.4.1	Telugu		94.75	92.84
CMATERdb 3.1.1 + ISI Oriya	Bangla + Oriya (Mixed)		92.68	92.66

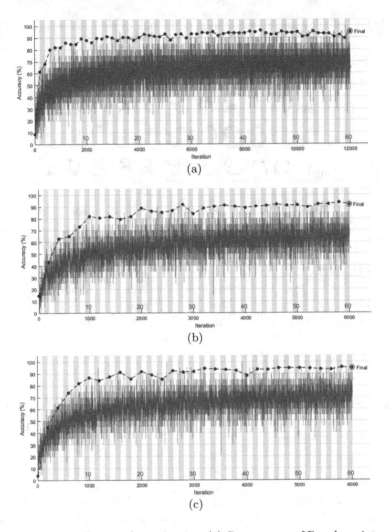

Fig. 3. Recognition efficiency determination. (a) Convergence of Bangla script employing Alexnet at 60 epoch; (b) Convergence of Devanagari script employing Alexnet at 60 epoch; (c) Convergence of Telugu script employing Alexnet at 60 epoch.

methodology. We were able to achieve a better result for Alexnet than VGG-16 in all the scripts used for experimentation. When VGG-16 is used, we achieved the highest accuracy of 93.33% for Bangla and Devanagari script and a lowest accuracy of 92.66% for mixed Bangla-Oriya script. Similarly, for Alexnet, we achieved a highest accuracy of 95.00% for Bangla script and a lowest accuracy of 91.72% for Devanagari script. We achieved a satisfactory accuracy of 92.68% and 92.66% when experimented on the mixed Bangla-Oriya script employing Alexnet and VGG-16 respectively. A detailed report is provided in Table 3. The convergence rate of Bangla, Devanagari, and Telugu while using Alexnet for 60 epoch is delineated in Fig. 3. For the application part, we have used the CMA-TERdb 3.1.1 Bangla dataset for training. We obtained an accuracy of 94.26% and 92.21% as the final result for Alexnet and VGG-16 respectively. Table 4 provides a detailed report. There are several works in the literature e.g. [26,27], etc, that have achieved higher accuracies than the presently proposed method. The aim of this work is to delineate the effectiveness of transfer learning and how a pre-trained model created for recognising natural images can be used to recognise handwritten numeral images.

Table 4. Detailed report of the extraction and recognition of Bangla pin codes from post cards.

# Postcards	Total # Digits	Correctly extracted	Training Set	Accuracy (%)	
				Alexnet	VGG-16
28	168	159	CMATERdb 3.1.1	94.26	92.21

4   Conclusion

There is a need for research and development on the automation for the recognition of handwritten forms and documents. The need is severe for a multilingual and developing country like India. The present work delineated a 3 fold study: Utilisation of pre-trained CNN architectures on four different Indic scripts, viz. Bangla, Devanagari, Oriya, and Telugu to achieve a satisfactory recognition rate, studying the performance of transfer learning on a Indic mixed script of Bangla and Oriya, and as a part of practical application, we have applied the aforementioned approach to recognize Bangla handwritten pin codes after their extraction from postal letters. We hope to study further how the mixing of more than two script would work when transfer learning is applied in the future.

References

1. Mahalat, M.H., Mollah, A.F., Basu, S., Nasipuri, M.: Design of novel post-processing algorithms for handwritten Arabic numerals classification. Int. J. Appl. Pattern Recognit. **4**(4), 342–357 (2017)
2. Prasad, B.K., Sanyal, G.: Novel features and a cascaded classifier based Arabic numerals recognition system. Multidimension. Syst. Signal Process. **29**(1), 321–338 (2018)
3. Zhang, X.Y., Bengio, Y., Liu, C.L.: Online and offline handwritten Chinese character recognition: a comprehensive study and new benchmark. Pattern Recognit. **61**, 348–360 (2017)
4. Niu, X.X., Suen, C.Y.: A novel hybrid CNN-SVM classifier for recognizing handwritten digits. Pattern Recognit. **45**(4), 1318–1325 (2012)

5. Ouchtati, S., Redjimi, M., Bedda, M.: Realization of an offline system for the recognition of the handwritten numeric chains. In: Proceedings of the Iberian Conference on Information Systems and Technologies, pp. 1–6 (2014)

6. Chakraborty, D., Pramanik, R., Bag, S.: A novel approach towards segmentation of connected handwritten numerals. In: Proceedings of the International Conference on Image Information Processing, pp. 1–5 (2017)

7. Singh, P.K., Sarkar, R., Nasipuri, M.: Offline script identification from multilingual Indic-script documents: a state-of-the-art. Comput. Sci. Rev. **15**, 1–28 (2015)

8. Pramanik, R., Bag, S.: Shape decomposition-based handwritten compound character recognition for Bangla OCR. J. Vis. Commun. Image Represent. **50**, 123–134 (2018)

9. Khan, H.A., Al Helal, A., Ahmed, K.I.: Handwritten Bangla digit recognition using sparse representation classifier. In: Proceedings of the International Conference on Informatics, Electronics and Vision, pp. 1–6 (2014)

10. Hassan, T., Khan, H.A.: Handwritten Bangla numeral recognition using local binary pattern. In: Proceedings of the International Conference on Electrical Engineering and Information Communication Technology, pp. 1–4 (2015)

11. Sarkhel, R., Das, N., Saha, A.K., Nasipuri, M.: A multi-objective approach towards cost effective isolated handwritten Bangla character and digit recognition. Pattern Recognit. **58**, 172–189 (2016)

12. Singh, P., Verma, A., Chaudhari, N.S.: Feature selection based classifier combination approach for handwritten Devanagari numeral recognition. Sadhana **40**(6), 1701–1714 (2015)

13. Prabhanjan, S., Dinesh, R.: Handwritten Devanagari numeral recognition by fusion of classifiers. Int. J. Signal Process. Image Process. Pattern Recognit. **8**(7), 41–50 (2015)

14. Roy, K., Pal, T., Pal, U., Kimura, F.: Oriya handwritten numeral recognition system. In: Proceedings of the International Conference on Document Analysis and Recognition, pp. 770–774 (2005)

15. Bhowmik, T.K., Parui, S.K., Bhattacharya, U., Shaw, B.: An HMM based recognition scheme for handwritten Oriya numerals. In: Proceedings of the International Conference on Information Technology, pp. 105–110 (2006)

16. Shopon, M., Mohammed, N., Abedin, M.A.: Bangla handwritten digit recognition using autoencoder and deep convolutional neural network. In: Proceedings of the International Workshop on Computational Intelligence, pp. 64–68 (2016)

17. Alom, M.Z., Sidike, P., Taha, T.M., Asari, V.K.: Handwritten Bangla digit recognition using deep learning. arXiv preprint arXiv:1705.02680 (2017)

18. Bhattacharya, U., Chaudhuri, B.B.: Handwritten numeral databases of Indian scripts and multistage recognition of mixed numerals. IEEE Trans. Pattern Anal. Mach. Intell. **31**(3), 444–457 (2009)

19. Singh, P.K., Sarkar, R., Nasipuri, M.: A study of moment based features on handwritten digit recognition. Appl. Comput. Intell. Soft Comput. 1–17 (2016)

20. Maitra, D.S., Bhattacharya, U., Parui, S.K.: CNN based common approach to handwritten character recognition of multiple scripts. In: Proceedings of the International Conference on Document Analysis and Recognition, pp. 1021–1025 (2015)

21. Pan, S.J., Yang, Q.: A survey on transfer learning. IEEE Trans. Knowl. Data Eng. **22**(10), 1345–1359 (2010)

22. Krizhevsky, A., Sutskever, I., Hinton, G.E.: Imagenet classification with deep convolutional neural networks. In: Advances in Neural Information Processing Systems, pp. 1097–1105 (2012)

23. Simonyan, K., Zisserman, A.: Very deep convolutional networks for large-scale image recognition. arXiv preprint arXiv:1409.1556 (2014)
24. Pramanik, R., Bag, S.: Linear curve fitting-based headline estimation in handwritten words for indian scripts. In: Shankar, B.U., Ghosh, K., Mandal, D.P., Ray, S.S., Zhang, D., Pal, S.K. (eds.) PReMI 2017. LNCS, vol. 10597, pp. 116–123. Springer, Cham (2017). https://doi.org/10.1007/978-3-319-69900-4_15
25. Bhattacharya, U., Chaudhuri, B.B.: Databases for research on recognition of handwritten characters of Indian scripts. In: Proceedings of the International Conference on Document Analysis and Recognition, pp. 789–793 (2005)
26. Das, N., Sarkar, R., Basu, S., Kundu, M., Nasipuri, M., Basu, D.K.: A genetic algorithm based region sampling for selection of local features in handwritten digit recognition application. Appl. Soft Comput. **12**(5), 1592–1606 (2012)
27. Das, N., Reddy, J.M., Sarkar, R., Basu, S., Kundu, M., Nasipuri, M., Basu, D.K.: A statistical-topological feature combination for recognition of handwritten numerals. Appl. Soft Comput. **12**(8), 2486–2495 (2012)
28. Basu, S., Das, N., Sarkar, R., Kundu, M., Nasipuri, M., Basu, D.K.: A novel framework for automatic sorting of postal documents with multi-script address blocks. Pattern Recognit. **43**(10), 3507–3521 (2010)

Symbol Spotting in Offline Handwritten Mathematical Expressions

Ridhi Aggarwal[1], Gaurav Harit[1(✉)], and Anil Kumar Tiwari[2]

[1] Department of Computer Science and Engineering,
Indian Institute of Technology Jodhpur, Jodhpur, India
{pg201384012,gharit}@iitj.ac.in
[2] Department of Electrical Engineering, Indian Institute of Technology Jodhpur,
Jodhpur, India
akt@iitj.ac.in

Abstract. Recognition of touching characters in mathematical expressions is a challenging problem in the field of document image analysis. Various approaches for recognizing touching maths symbols have been reported in literature, but they mainly dealt with printed expressions and handwritten numeral strings. In this work, a new segmentation-free approach is proposed which matches convex shape portions of symbols occurring in various layout such as subscript, superscript, fraction etc. and is able to perform spotting of symbols present in a handwritten expression. Our contribution lies in the design of a novel feature which can handle touching symbols effectively in the presence of handwriting variations. This recognition-based approach helps in spotting symbols in an expression even in the presence of clutter created by the presence of other symbols.

1 Introduction

Symbols in mathematical expressions have varied spatial configurations. We attempt the problem of symbol spotting in mathematical expressions. A straight forward approach will be to segment the expression into component symbols and recognize the symbols. However segmentation of a handwritten mathematical expression is hard due to non-uniform spacing between the symbols and cases of overlap between neighbouring characters. There has been past work which has dealt with segmentation of neighbouring characters in handwritten words and numeral strings. But in case of mathematical expressions, the variability in the placement of symbols makes segmentation even more difficult. Essentially our problem resembles that of extracting symbols in a cluttered background where the clutter is attributed to the presence of other symbols and operators in the expression.

Automatic recognition of these mathematical expressions has been an important topic of research in pattern recognition and image analysis. The recognition of mathematical expressions in a document is substantially different from

S. Sundaram and G. Harit (Eds.): DAR 2018, CCIS 1020, pp. 52–64, 2019.
https://doi.org/10.1007/978-981-13-9361-7_5

the recognition of normal text. In normal text, the characters are systematically written from left to right while in mathematical expressions, the structural layout of characters is not fixed. Due to varied layout the characters can be touched in several ways. Much work has been reported for recognizing touching characters and the approaches can be broadly categorized as segmentation-based approach [8,9,11–13,15,16] and recognition-based [3,5]. However, these techniques mainly deal with printed expressions and handwritten numeral strings. Due to complex structure of expressions, the segmentation is not an easy task for touching characters in mathematical expressions. Printed expressions are more regular and constrained due to uniform spacing between characters. Handwritten expressions exhibit non-uniform spacing between adjacent symbols due to different writing styles and variability in handwriting of different people. So, to separate the touching characters, the segmentation of single-touching and multi-touching characters in handwritten numeral string is performed in [8]. Skeletons are obtained for the foreground and background regions of the image. To obtain the touching-pattern, the feature points on foreground and background skeletons are extracted. Fork-points, end-points, and corner-points are identified on the skeleton and used as feature points. Based on the location of these feature points, possible segmentation paths are constructed to separate the touching characters. Features capturing the geometric properties are analysed using a Gaussian Mixture Model to rank all the possible segmentation paths and select the best segmentation path.

An efficient way to evaluate the segmentation cuts has been proposed in [13]. The change in the concavity at the segmentation point is used to verify whether the segmentation cut is generating over-segmented characters or not. It was observed that compared to the segmentation of two dissimilar characters the (over-) segmentation of a single character would result in a change in concavity that remains similar across the segmentation point. Segmentation paths are also computed by using graph theory and heuristic rules [11]. The segmentation cut is computed by grouping edges and vertices into two disconnected sub-graphs using heuristics. The above approaches for segmenting handwritten digits [8,11,13] utilize thinning algorithm to convert the image into skeleton. Skeletonization often leads to information loss which may mislead the extraction of features.

To avoid Skeletonization, features for segmentation were directly extracted from the large-space,called reservoir, created between touching characters in a numeral string [6,7]. Features pertaining to the profile of the reservoir such as size and shape of the reservoir, number of reservoirs, boundary of reservoirs etc. are computed. The boundary of a reservoir signifies the touching line between the two characters. A limitation of this approach is that it works only for single touching point and the reservoir boundary should not contain any broken character. For multiple touching points, this approach was combined with the drop-fall algorithm [4]. Between two multiple touching characters, a closed loop is formed at touching points. Using information from neighbouring pixels, a segmentation path is defined for the closed loop. To evaluate whether the segmentation of touching characters is correct or not, the segmented character is recognized and

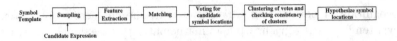

Fig. 1. Processing pipeline for symbol spotting

the feature vector is computed to find the similarity between the segmented character and the recognition result [14].

Apart from segmentation-based approach and recognition-based approach, Chatbri et al. [2] proposed a content-based retrieval system of handwritten queries in a document image. Using the contour points distribution histograms, the connected components of document image taht are similar to the connected components of query are located. However, this approach works only for the non-touching characters present in a document image.

A shape-based recognition approach was presented in [10] to recognize the touching characters in a handwritten word. To obtain the shape of the character in an image, a set of features are extracted which are collectively known as Gradient, Structural, Concavity (GSC) features. This feature set combines the gradient feature to find the stroke shape over short distance, structural feature to find the stroke trajectories over longer distances, and concavity features to detect stroke relationships over even longer distances which covers an entire image. Since, the concavity feature extracts the relationship of pixels at a larger scale, it is found to be stable in the presence of handwriting variations.

This paper consists of five sections. Section 2 introduces the proposed surround profile descriptor. Section 3 describes our approach (depicted in Fig. 1). The details of experiments along with analysis and discussion of results are reported in Sect. 4.2. Section 5 presents the concluding remarks.

1.1   Our Contributions

In this work we propose a new feature called the *surround profile* and use it for matching convex shape portions in the presence of clutter. The formulation of this feature is motivated from existing features such as the shape context [1] proposed for shape matching and the star like pattern [10] proposed for extracting concavity feature. There are shape detection frameworks such as contour context selection [17] which can be used to detect objects in cluttered images. However, such techniques are not directly applicable to symbol spotting because the model contour alignment can easily break down in the presence of handwriting variations.

Using the surround profile feature we develop a recognition-based technique for symbol spotting in handwritten mathematical expressions. It is well known that convexity of shapes within handwritten characters remains quite robust to variations in handwriting (see Fig. 2). We therefore make use of convex patterns as important features to help in symbol spotting. The approach is a segmentation-free approach and works well with varied layouts of symbols in handwritten mathematical expressions.

Fig. 2. Convexity of shapes in different handwritten characters indicated by red arrows. Closed regions indicated by red dots. (Color figure online)

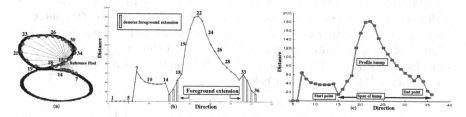

Fig. 3. Shape Descriptor: (a) Black Pixels, (b) Foreground extension, and (c) Profile Hump

2   The Surround Profile Descriptor

The proposed shape descriptor captures the relative positions of the black (foreground) pixels which are closest along each direction as shown in Fig. 3. Consider a reference pixel p at which the shape descriptor is to be computed. We consider 36 discretized directions around the pixel. The distance of the closest black pixel along each direction is noted. However, if the closest black pixel is one of the 8 neighbours of the reference pixel then we set a boolean flag entry to record a *foreground extension* along that direction and also record the run length (beginning from reference pixel) of foreground pixels along that direction. The surround profile can be conveniently represented using two arrays:

- A boolean array of flag value to indicate presence/absence of foreground extension for each direction.
- A scalar array of numbers where an entry can indicate
  - the distance of the black pixel from p if the corresponding boolean array entry does not indicate foreground extension.
  - the run length of foreground black pixel starting from p along that direction if the corresponding boolean array entry indicates foreground extension.

The surround profile can be wrapped around i.e. the profile value at 360 degree is the same as the profile value at 0 degree.

Figure 3 illustrates an example computation of this descriptor. When the reference pixel is partially surrounded by a convex shape the corresponding region of the surround profile gets a hump. Such profile humps are robust to handwriting variations. The span of a hump is given by the starting and ending directions. Foreground extensions can occur at the start/end of a hump.

Matching of two surround profiles sp_1 and sp_2 is done as follows:

1. Locate the profile humps in the surround profile sp_1.
2. A hump h_1 in sp_1 is considered to have a matching hump h_2 in sp_2 if both h_1 and h_2 have similar starting and ending angles and matching presence of foreground extensions at hump boundaries (start/end directions). Let $\triangle_s$ be the difference between the starting angles of h_1 and h_2. Let $\triangle_e$ be the difference between the ending angles of h_1 and h_2. Let fgs_1 and fgs_2 indicate presence of foreground extension at the start of h_1 and h_2 respectively. Let fge_1 and fge_2 indicate presence of foreground extension at the end of h_1 and h_2 respectively. The match measure is computed as a product of three components (1), (2), (3) given below:

$$\frac{1}{2}\left[1 - min\left(\frac{\triangle_s}{\triangle_m}, 1\right) + 1 - min\left(\frac{\triangle_e}{\triangle_m}, 1\right)\right] \tag{1}$$

$$\text{match}(fgs_1, fgs_2) \tag{2}$$

$$\text{match}(fge_1, fge_2) \tag{3}$$

Here $\triangle_m$ is a threshold for maximum allowable angle mismatch, fixed to $30°$. To get the maximum number of correct matching humps, it is very important to set the optimum value of $\triangle_m$. If value of $\triangle_m$ is increased, more number of inappropriate matches will occur as larger deviations in the sizes of the matching hump will get acceptable. The function $\text{match}(fgs_1, fgs_2)$ returns 1 if foreground extension has a matching status (present or absent) at the starting points of both h_1 and h_2. If the status does not match then this function returns 0.75 (as penalty).
Likewise $\text{match}(fge_1, fge_2)$ checks for matching status of foreground extension for end points.
The value of match measure ranges from 0 to 1. The match measure value '1' denotes that hump h_1 of sp_1 completely matches to hump h_2 of sp_2.
3. If there are multiple profile humps in sp_1 then an aggregated match score of all the profile humps can be computed as the average/max/min of the match scores of all the humps, or we can select the match score for the largest spanning (prominent) hump. In this work we take the latter approach so as to make the matching more robust to handwriting variations.

A unique feature of the matching procedure is that there may be additional profile humps in sp_2 which do not have a match with any profile hump in sp_1. Such additional humps do not interfere with the match score and they are attributed to the clutter arising due to presence of other symbols in the neighbourhood. However, there is also a possibility that profile humps arising due to clutter can have a good match with a profile hump of sp_1. Such incorrect matches can be detected and their influence can be minimized using validity checks as explained in Sect. 3.4.

3 Methodology

This section describes the processing steps involved in our symbol spotting framework (see Fig. 1). The input to the system is an image of a symbol template and a candidate expression image in which the symbol needs to be searched. The first step is to obtain sample points on both the symbol template and the candidate expression. The input image is binarized and points are sampled on both the symbol template and candidate expression.

3.1 Image Sampling

Image sampling is done by following the three steps given below:

1. Sampling along a horizontal scan
   - Consider a row r with a contiguous run of black pixels starting at the ith pixel and having a run length L.
   - If L exceeds a threshold τ, then we find the mid point on the run as $i + \frac{L}{2}$. Except for the one pixel close to the mid point the rest of the pixels on the run are converted to white (background).
2. Sampling along a vertical scan: This is similar to the horizontal scan.
3. Sampling using a sliding window: A sliding window of size $m \times m$ is moved over the image. If the centre pixel of the window is foreground then all other foreground pixels (except for the center pixel) within the window are converted to background. The results obtained after this step are shown in Fig. 4. If the window size m is increased, more number of pixels in the window are converted to background and hence, less number of sample points are obtained. Similarly, if the window size is decreased, less number of pixels in the window are converted to background which may result in redundant sample points. Hence, the size of sliding window is required to be fixed to achieve an optimum number of sample points. The sampling procedure does not require the input image to be skeletonized. The surround profile is computed on these sample points to spot the symbol in an expression.

3.2 Recognizing a Symbol Within an Expression

Consider a given template of a symbol t_s and a candidate expression c_e which is likely to contain a symbol s. The task is to find the possible locations of the symbol template t_s in the expression.

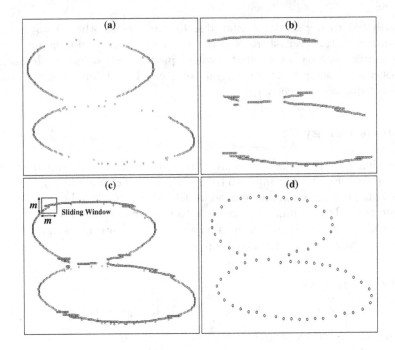

Fig. 4. Image sampling: (a) Horizontal scan, (b) Vertical scan, (c) Sampling using sliding window, and (d) Output

1. Sample the symbol template and the expression.
2. Compute the surround profile descriptor on each sample point.
3. Use the surround profile descriptor to match each sample point on t_s with the sample points on c_e.

Lets say sp_1 is the surround profile of a point on symbol template. Consider sp_2 as a descriptor computed for a sample point on the candidate expression. The match score values are computed between sp_1 and descriptor values sp_2's computed at all the sample points. The sample points on the candidate expression that gives the closest match is taken as the match for reference point p. This is how we get a set of point matches. Since there can be some humps arising due to clutter, this can lead to accidental matching of a hump on sp_1 with a hump (due to clutter) on sp_2. But because the matching process seeks to match humps in sp_1, the humps arising due to clutter in sp_2 get ignored most of the time and do not interfere.

Once we have point matches we need to: (i) identify the set of matches that hypothesize the presence of the symbol and (ii) reject the mismatches. This is achieved by verifying the spatial consistency of the matching points as explained in the next section.

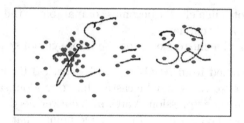

Fig. 5. Location of votes hypothesizes location of symbol centroid for query symbol 'x'

3.3   Voting for Candidate Locations of the Symbol

For every sample point st_i on the symbol template we note the vector pointing to the centroid. Each matched point on the candidate expression casts its vote towards candidate centroid locations of the symbol in the expression (see Fig. 5). The sample point st_i has vector h_i pointing to the symbol centroid in the template and if it matches with multiple sample points ce_{j1}, ce_{j2}, etc. on the expression then all these matches will cast separate votes for the presence of a symbol centroid at offset h_i w.r.t. themselves. Along with the vote we also store the strength of the vote which is proportional to the match strength. Once all the sample points on the symbol template have been matched to sample points on the expression, the votes casted indicate the possible locations for the symbol centroid on that expression. Regions with higher density of votes indicate the presence of symbol. The votes are clustered to obtain the candidate locations with higher density of votes. We make use of agglomerative hierarchical clustering (AHC) which unlike k-means can find variable number of clusters depending on the stopping criteria that govern cluster agglomeration. We adopt the following stopping criteria:

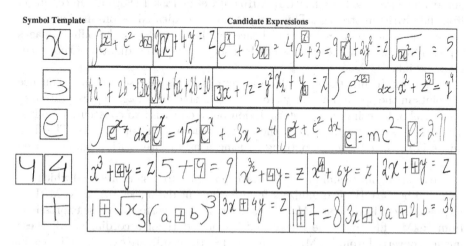

Fig. 6. Example results of symbol spotting. The leftmost column shows the symbol template used for spotting. For spotting '4' we used two symbol templates.

1. The number of votes in a cluster becomes comparable to the number of sample points on the symbol template.
2. Distance between the clusters exceeds the inter-symbol spacing.

The clusters obtained from AHC need to be checked for validity (appropriateness). This is because votes may be casted due to random sample matches on the other symbols in the expression. Votes in a cluster need not be all correct. The correct votes are the ones casted by sample points that belong to an actually present correct symbol, and the incorrect votes are those casted by random matches to sample points on the incorrect symbols (forming the clutter).

3.4 Cluster Validity Check

For each vote in a cluster we get the sample point once which casted that vote and track the corresponding match point in the symbol template. This match point on the symbol template is marked. Once all the votes of the cluster have been processed in this way we get some marked portions on the symbol template. This in turn can identify portions of the symbol template that have not been marked. If more than 50% sample points on the symbol template have not been marked it means that the cluster contains centroids that do not strongly indicate evidence of the presence of the symbol at that location. Only the votes having adequate strength (> 0.6) are used for cluster validity check.

4 Dataset and Experimentation

4.1 Dataset

Since any standard public dataset of handwritten mathematical expressions is not available, we use the CROHME 2016 dataset of Task-1 (Formula Recognition from handwritten strokes). This competition is dedicated to on-line handwritten mathematical expressions and hence, we have produced the offline images representing these online expressions by using the x-y co-ordinates of the traces made by ink.

In an InkML file, the symbols in an expression is represented as a sequence of points in the space. For every sroke, we rendered the image representation of each symbol by using linear interpolation between each two consecutive points. Then the line is drawn between these two consecutive stroke points. The final image is produced after smoothing it using a mean filter with a window sized 3×3 pixels.

To evaluate our technique, 8,836 mathematical expressions are used which are collected by CROHME organizers from 5 different databases:HAMEX, MfrDB, ExpressMatch, KAIST and MathBrush. We have converted all these expressions from InkML file to offline image and annotated them accordingly. All these images converted from InkML files are used as the candidate expression image in which the symbol needs to be searched. Also, the symbol templates for all the 101 symbol classes are created separately. The CROHME dataset has a very small number (only 55) of expressions that have touching characters. Therefore we have created our own dataset of offline handwritten expressions with more examples of touching characters. We have collected a set of 25 expressions which contain 2 to 8 symbols. Each of these 25 expressions was written by 10 different writers on a paper resulting in a set of 250 expression documents. These documents were scanned at 300dpi on HP scanner.

4.2 Results

The precision and recall is computed to evaluate the spotting performance of our proposed method. We compared our work with the well known shape context descriptor. The comparison on symbol spotting performance with shape context descriptor and proposed descriptor on both datasets is presented in Table 1. It is found that the point correspondences obtained by using the shape context descriptor are distracted due to the clutter and hence are scattered all over the math expression image (Fig. 8). Therefore, it does not offer good symbol localization properties.

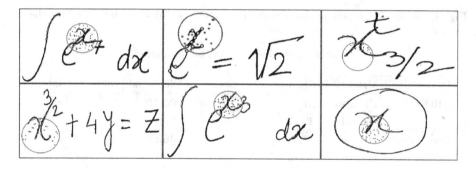

Fig. 7. Recognizing touching character x in various handwriting using surround profile descriptor

On the CROHME dataset, the proposed approach achieved a better precision of 96.10% and 100% recall thereby demonstrating its robustness to handwriting variations. The similar looking symbols such as {4, y}, {0, O, o}, {1, l}, {g, 9} are difficult to differentiate in a handwritten document and hence, leads to 96.10% precision value. The results of symbol spotting are illustrated in Fig. 6. The matched symbol is marked by the bounding box in candidate expression. Since the convexity of shapes within handwritten characters remains quite robust to handwriting variations, the symbol x written by different writers in various layout (subscript, superscript, and baseline) is also spotted in spite of the clutter created by the presence of other symbols, as shown in Fig. 7. The experiment is repeated on the same expressions using the shape context descriptor but it fails to spot the symbol x correctly as shown in (Fig. 8).

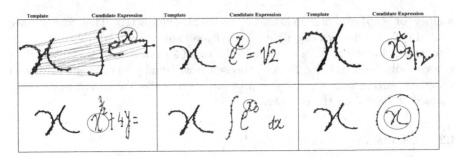

Fig. 8. Recognizing touching character x in various handwriting using shape context descriptor

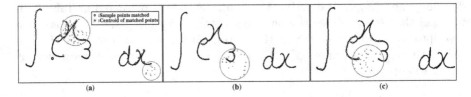

Fig. 9. Recognizing touching characters: (a) character x, (b) character 3, and (c) character e

Table 1. Symbol spotting performance

Dataset	Metric(%)	Shape context descriptor	Surround profile descriptor
CROHME	**Precision**	31.44	**96.10**
	Recall	39.25	**100**
Our Dataset	**Precision**	27.34	**96.65**
	Recall	30.76	**100**

The descriptor results in a successful matching in the presence of minor size variations. However, experiments have showed that for a larger sized symbol or a very small sized symbol, the votes can get spread sparsely across a larger region. In Fig. 9 it can be seen that the vote cluster for symbol e is slightly drifted away from the actual symbol e. This happened because the template used for e is larger in scale compared to the instance of e appearing in the expression. Nevertheless it was spotted correctly because the cluster was assessed to be valid.

Matching using surround profile is also susceptible to give false detections for similar looking symbols like 4 and y in Fig. 10. Hence, for a given query of symbol 4, two symbols are spotted: symbol 4 and symbol y. Though, matching score of symbol 4 is higher, the matching score of symbol y also satisfies the threshold for cluster validity. For symbols such as 4, we include two types of templates as shown in Fig. 6.

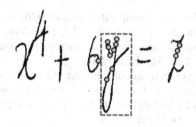

Fig. 10. Part of symbol y matches with part of symbol 4's template

5   Conclusions

In this paper we presented a recognition based technique for symbol spotting in handwritten mathematical expressions. We proposed a new feature called the *surround profile* and use it for matching convex shape portions of symbols in the presence of clutter. The proposed surround profile descriptor works well with various layouts of symbols in an expression. Touching symbols are detected in the presence of handwriting variations.

References

1. Belongie, S., Malik, J., Puzicha, J.: Shape context: a new descriptor for shape matching and object recognition. In: NIPS (2000)
2. Chatbri, H., Kameyama, K., Kwan, P.: Towards a segmentation and recognition-free approach for content-based document image retrieval of handwritten queries. In: 2015 3rd IAPR Asian Conference on Pattern Recognition (ACPR), pp. 146–150. IEEE (2015)
3. Garain, U., Chaudhuri, B.: Segmentation of touching symbols for OCR of printed mathematical expressions: an approach based on multifactorial analysis. In: ICDAR, pp. 177–181. IEEE (2005)
4. Ma, R., Zhao, Y., Xia, Y., Yan, Y.: A touching pattern-oriented strategy for handwritten digits segmentation. In: Computational Intelligence and Security 2008, CIS 2008. vol. 1, pp. 174–179. IEEE (2008)
5. Nomura, A., Michishita, K., Uchida, S., Suzuki, M.: Detection and segmentation of touching characters in mathematical expressions. In: ICDAR, pp. 126–130. IEEE (2003)
6. Pal, U., Belaïd, A., Choisy, C.: Touching numeral segmentation using water reservoir concept. Pattern Recogn. Lett. **24**(1), 261–272 (2003)
7. Pal, U., Belaïd, A., Choisy, C.: Water reservoir based approach for touching numeral segmentation. In: ICDAR, pp. 892–896. IEEE (2001)
8. Sadri, J., Suen, C.Y., Bui, T.D.: Automatic segmentation of unconstrained handwritten numeral strings. In: IWFHR, pp. 317–322. IEEE (2004)
9. Shrivastava, D., Sinha, R., Saraswat, S., Gupta, H.P., Dutta, T.: A mathematical equation solving system using accelerometer sensor. In: 10th International Conference on Communication Systems & Networks (COMSNETS) 2018, pp. 388–391. IEEE (2018)

10. Srikantan, J.F.G., Srihari, S.: Handprinted character/digit recognition using a multiple feature/resolution philosophy. In: ICFHR, pp. 57–66 (1994)
11. Suwa, M.: Segmentation of connected handwritten numerals by graph representation. In: ICDAR, pp. 750–754. IEEE (2005)
12. Tian, X., Zhang, Y.: Segmentation of touching characters in mathematical expressions using contour feature technique. In: Software Engineering, Artificial Intelligence, Networking, and Parallel/Distributed Computing 2007, SNPD 2007. Eighth ACIS. vol. 1, pp. 206–209. IEEE (2007)
13. Vellasques, E., Oliveira, L.S., Britto, A.d.S., Koerich, A.L., Sabourin, R.: Filtering segmentation cuts for digit string recognition. Pattern Recogn. **41**(10), 3044–3053 (2008)
14. Wang, Y., Liu, X., Jia, Y.: Statistical modeling and learning for recognition-based handwritten numeral string segmentation. In: ICDAR, pp. 421–425. IEEE (2009)
15. Yoo, Y.H., Kim, J.H.: Mathematical formula recognition based on modified recursive projection profile cutting and labeling with double linked list. In: Kim, J.H., Matson, E., Myung, H., Xu, P. (eds.) Robot Intelligence Technology and Applications 2012. Advances in Intelligent Systems and Computing, pp. 983–992. Springer, Heidelberg (2013). https://doi.org/10.1007/978-3-642-37374-9_95
16. Zanibbi, R., Yu, L.: Math spotting: retrieving math in technical documents using handwritten query images. In: 2011 International Conference on Document Analysis and Recognition (ICDAR), pp. 446–451. IEEE (2011)
17. Zhu, Q., Wang, L., Wu, Y., Shi, J.: Contour context selection for object detection: a set-to-set contour matching approach. In: Forsyth, D., Torr, P., Zisserman, A. (eds.) ECCV 2008. LNCS, vol. 5303, pp. 774–787. Springer, Heidelberg (2008). https://doi.org/10.1007/978-3-540-88688-4_57

Online Handwritten Bangla Character Recognition Using Frechet Distance and Distance Based Features

Shibaprasad Sen[1(✉)], Jewel Chakraborty[1], Snehanjan Chatterjee[1], Rohit Mitra[1], Ram Sarkar[2], and Kaushik Roy[3]

[1] Future Institute of Engineering and Management, Kolkata, India
shibubiet@gmail.com, jewelchakraborty3@gmail.com, snehanjan.29@gmail.com,
rmartimtihor@gmail.com
[2] Jadavpur University, Kolkata, India
raamsarkar@gmail.com
[3] West Bengal State University, Barasat, India
kaushik.mrg@gmail.com

Abstract. This paper inspects the impact of feature vector produced by Frechet Distance (FD) along with the conventional distance based features to recognize online handwritten Bangla characters. FD based feature computation starts with dividing a character sample into different rectangular zones. Then FD values are computed from each zone to every other zones. In distance based feature extraction technique also a character sample is divided into several segments and distances are measured from a particular segment to all other segments. Feature vectors so produced are experimented on 10000 online handwritten Bangla characters. SVM (Support Vector Machine) classifier produces the reasonably satisfactory recognition accuracy of 98.98% when FD based features are combined with distance based features.

Keywords: Frechet distance · Online handwriting recognition ·
Distance based feature · Classification · SVM

1 Introduction

With the evolution of modern electronic devices and the improvement in internet facilities, the demand for a better and easy life has reached to its peak. Devices like tablets, A4 Take Note, smart phones, iPad, etc. are dominating today's digital world due to easy availability and affordability of the same. These technological advancements give rise some new research topics and help in popularizing some less explored research topics. Online Handwriting Recognition (OHR) is an forthcoming research area which takes the full advantages of this changing need of the digital world. People nowadays are becoming more used to in writing information freely in their normal style on the said electronic devices. An added advantage of this new trend is that supplied data on those devices are saved

S. Sundaram and G. Harit (Eds.): DAR 2018, CCIS 1020, pp. 65–73, 2019.
https://doi.org/10.1007/978-981-13-9361-7_6

as online information (timely ordered pixels with pen up and down information). Numerous publications are found in the literature for the texts written in
Devanagari, English, Gurumukhi scripts [1–8]. In counterpart for Bangla script,
number of available research works is limited. Bag et al. have mentioned an
approach for the recognition of characters irrespective of writing direction [9].
Another direction towards character recognition is addressed by Roy et al. [10].
This strategy finds constituent strokes from characters. Sequential and dynamic
information are collected at stroke level and used as features for stroke recognition. Authors have formed character from the stroke sequences by matching with
previously built rule base. In [11], authors have highlighted the efficiency of direction code features towards recognition of online Bangla characters. Authors in
[12] have collected constituent strokes from characters and arranged them into 54
classes according to the shape similarity. An individual HMM has been designed
for each stroke class. Characters are then formed from recognized strokes by
taking the help of 50 look up tables. Authors in [13–15] have reflected the effectiveness of HD (Hausdorff distance) based features, area feature, chord length,
mass distribution and direction along with point-float features towards character
recognition. Sen et al. have reported the impact of extracted distance based features [16], global information and local information [17] to recognize handwritten
characters. Authors have shown the effectiveness of structural and topological
features to recognized basic Bangla characters in [18]. Bandyopadhyay et al. have
directed stroke-based character recognition methodology in [19] where individual stroke is described by shape based features. DTW (Dynamic Time Warping)
technique has been used for recognition of a stroke by matching with already
prepared stroke database. Authors in [20] have recognized the component strokes
of characters by using combined ZPT (Zone based path traversal) with distance
based features. Resultant character is then formed from recognized strokes using
DFA based procedure.

After deeply analyzing the above mentioned research works, it has been
noticed that though few research attempts had been made to recognize Bangla
characters, there are still more scopes to enhance the overall performance by
improving recognition accuracy by distinguishing similar shaped characters.
Therefore, in this paper, the importance of FD features combined with distance
based features is emphasized to recognize Bangla characters.

2   Database Preparation and Pre-processing

Variation among the data present in a database is a basic need to assess the
strength of any algorithm in the domain of handwriting recognition. Keeping
this issue in mind, 100 persons belonging to different age group with varied
educational and social background, sex etc. are made involved during the data
collection process. As, there are 50 distinct symbols in the Bangla alphabet,
hence a database constituting 10000 character symbols has been prepared under
this work. No strict burden were forced on the contributors. In this experiment,
pre-processing stages like point normalization and size normalization follow the

same procedures as mentioned in [13]. In this experiment, each character is normalized into 64 points and scaled in a window of size 512×512.

3 Feature Extraction

Two different feature vectors termed as FD and distance based, are extracted under the present work and applied to recognize the isolated Bangla characters. Following sub-sections describe the detailed feature extraction procedures.

3.1 FD Based Feature

For the computation of FD based features, a sample character is divided into N number of zones as reflected in Fig. 1. Then FDs of pixel points from one zone to every other zones are computed and these distance values act as features for the current experiment. Forward FD (FFD), termed as f(P, Q), from zone P to zone Q is computed by using Eq. 1.

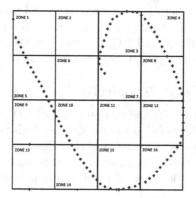

Fig. 1. Image of a character when divided into 16 zones.

$$f(P,Q) = \begin{array}{c} \min_{a,b}[\max\{d(P(a) - Q(b))\}] \\ a[0, N] \leftarrow a[0, 1] \\ b[0, M] \leftarrow b[0, 1] \end{array} \tag{1}$$

where a and b refers the numbers of pixels belong to zone P and zone Q respectively. For the present experiment, distance d is considered as the Euclidian distance. The FFD computation from zone 1 to zone 7 is demonstrated in Fig. 2(a–b). Green colored lines in (a), denote the measurement of maximum distance from each point of zone 1 to every other points in zone 7. The minimum of all those maximum distances is then considered as FFD from zone 1 to zone 7 and is shown in Fig. 2(b) by red colored line.

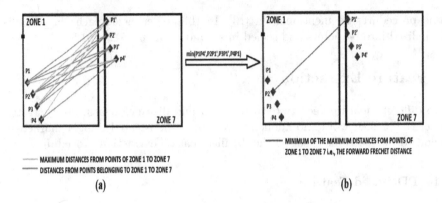

Fig. 2. (a–b) FFD computation from zone 1 to zone 7. (Color figure online)

The same procedure is applied to compute Backward FD (BFD), f(Q, P) from the pixels belonging to zone Q to zone P. The BFD computation from zone 7 to zone 1 is illustrated in Fig. 3(a–b).

FD between any two zones is considered as the minimum of FFD and BFD. The computed FD values between two zones may exhibit asymmetric property because the value of f(P, Q) and f(Q, P) may not be always same. FD measurement between zones P and Q, takes the minimum of f(P, Q) and f(Q, P) as reflected in Eq. 2.

$$FD(P,Q) = min(f(P,Q), f(Q,p)) \tag{2}$$

The detailed procedure for the computation of FD based features is mentioned in Algorithm 1. In this algorithm α denotes high positive value.

From Algorithm 1, it has been observed that FD based technique tries to find the similarity of the shapes of the character components belonging to different zones by computing the distances of pixel points between these two zones. It

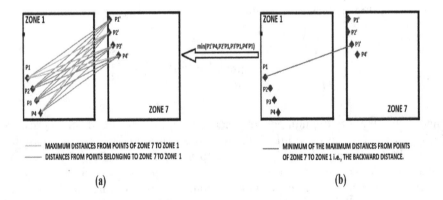

Fig. 3. (a–b) BFD computation from zone 7 to zone 1.

has also been noticed that few zones may present there, that do not have data pixel in it. As a result, this technique generates N X (N−1)/2 number of FD values from a character sample that are considered as feature values. Therefore, a total of 6, 36, 120, 300 features are generated respectively when the character is divided into 4, 9, 16 and 25 zones.

4   Experimental Results

In this experiment, two different feature extraction strategies called FD and distance based have been experimented to recognize online Bangla characters. The combined effect of these two features have also been experimented under this work. Table 1 reflects the dimension of all the different feature sets used in present work. These feature vectors are fed to five well-known classifiers viz., SVM (Support Vector Machine), BayesNet, NaiveBayes, MLP (Multilayer Perceptron) and Simple Logistic. 5-fold cross validation scheme is applied for classification purpose. Table 2 highlights the recognition accuracies obtained for FD based features of different dimensions. This table records the recognition accuracies produced by the above mentioned classifiers on 10000 character datasets. It has been noticed from Table 2 that increasing the number of divisions (from 4 to 16), recognition accuracy gradually increases. This is because of producing more number of segments as number of division increases. The extracted features from those segments in turn becomes more effective for the recognition of the character. As an effect, the FD based features produce highest recognition accuracy of 93.06% by SVM classifier for 16 zones and this entry is marked by Grey colored cell in Table 2. It is noticed that when the number of divisions of the character is further increased to 25 zones, then the recognition accuracy starts decreasing. This is because, the length of segmented components becomes so small that the extracted features from it becomes less informative.

The distance based feature extraction technique mentioned in [16] was experimented with the values of N = 6, 8, 10, 16, 32, 40, 48, 52, 55 and reveals that highest recognition was achieved when the value of N was set to 16. Hence, in the present work, the value of N is set to 16 and with this value highest recognition accuracy of 98.20% is reflected by SVM classifier.

Furthermore, the features produced by FD (for 16 zones) and distance based (16 segment) techniques are combined and then the combined feature vector is reduced to 77 attribute by applying PCA. The resultant feature vector is fed to before mentioned classifiers for recognition purpose. In this situation also SVM scores the highest accuracy of 98.98%. Clearly this accuracy is better than the individual impact obtained from both FD based and distance based technique.

Figure 4 depicts the performance of all the classifiers for FD, distance based and combination of FD and distance based features. Blue, orange and grey colored lines represent FD, distance based and combination of FD and distance based features respectively. This can be noted from Fig. 4 that grey colored line always lies in top for all the classifiers and for every zone.

ALGORITHM 1. FD calculation between the curves belonging to any two zones

---

1. FFD = α, BFD = α
2. for each point i=1 to N of P
2.1. max=0
2.2. for each point j=1 to M of Q,
2.3. if i!=j then
2.3.1.k[i,j]=d(i,j)//distance from i^{th} point to j^{th} point
2.3.2. if k[i,j]>max then
2.3.2.1. max=k[i,j]
2.4. End of for
2.5. if FFD>max then
2.5.1. FFD =max //forward Frechet distance
2.6. End of for
3. for each point j=1 to M of Q
3.1. max=0
3.2. for each point i=1 to N of P
3.3. if i!=j then
3.3.1.k[j,i]=d(j,i)//distance from j^{th} point to i^{th} point
3.3.2.if k[j,i]>max then
3.3.2.1 max=k[j,i]
3.4. End of for
3.5. if BFD>max then
3.5.1. BFD=max //backward Frechet distance
3.6.End of for
4. if FFD<BFD then
4.1. FD = FFD
5. else
5.1. FD = BFD

Table 1. Illustration of feature set and their combination used in the present work

Features used	Number of image segments	#Feature dimension
FD based	4	6
	9	36
	16	120
	25	300
Distance based	16	120

Though the combined feature vector efficiently distinguishes different character symbols, still few character pairs are misclassified with each other due to almost similar shape structure, which are highlighted in Table 3. A comparative

Table 2. Recognition accuracies shown by the classifiers for FD based feature extraction technique

Classifier	Success rate (in %)			
	Number of zones			
	4	9	16	25
BayesNet	47.83	78.63	86.68	86.98
SVM	41.50	86.57	**93.06**	91.28
Simple Logistic	42.33	84.89	92.73	90.22
MLP	56.91	83.68	89.49	89.47
Naive Bayes	44.26	55.76	78.26	84.40

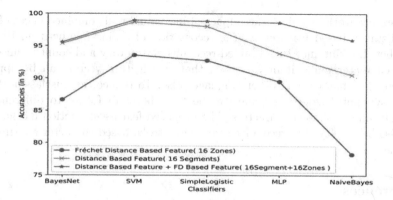

Fig. 4. The performance of classifiers for FD based features, distance based features and combination of those. (Color figure online)

Table 3. Most misclassified character pairs

Misclassified character pairs	# samples misclassified (out of 200)
,	5
,	3
,	5
,	3

analysis with some past works has been illustrated in Table 4 in order to emphasize the effectiveness of the proposed feature extraction strategy. The features mentioned through [10–13] done on our dataset for comparison purpose.

Table 4. Comparison of the proposed procedure with few past research works

Reference	Used features	Accuracy (in %)
[10]	Structural + Point based	94.8
[12]	Shape Based Feature (Shape and Size of stroke)	93.05
[13]	Hausdorff distance based	95.57
[11]	Direction code	94.92
Proposed technique	FD based	93.06
	Distance based	98.20
	FD + Distance based	98.98

5   Conclusion

The present work examines the impact of individual and combined effect of FD and distance based features for the recognition of online handwritten Bangla alphabet. Looking into the obtained recognition accuracy and count of misclassified character pairs, it may be said that this feature vector can be applied to recognize characters of other languages also. To reduce the misclassification, a non-symmetric zoning scheme can be thought of in future to differentiate strongly similar shaped characters. The proposed feature extraction mechanism can also be employed to recognize strokes for stroke-based character recognition scheme.

References

1. Connell, S.D., Sinha, R.M.K., Jain, A.K.: Recognition of unconstrained online Devenagari characters. In: 15th International Conference on Pattern Recognition, pp. 368–371 (2000)
2. Joshi, N., Sita, G., Ramakrishnan, A.G., Deepu, V.: Machine recognition of online handwritten Devanagari characters. In: Proceedings of International Conference on Document Analysis and Recognition, pp. 1156–1160 (2005)
3. Ahmed, B.B., Naz, S., Razzak, M.I., Rashid, S.F., Afzal, M.Z., Breuel, T.M.: Evaluation of cursive and non-cursive scripts using recurrent neural networks. Int. J. Neural Comput. Appl. **27**(3), 603–613 (2016)
4. Bahlmann, C., Burkhardt, H.: The writer independent online handwriting recognition system frog on hand and cluster generative statistical dynamic time warping. IEEE Trans. Pattern Anal. Mach. Intell. **26**(3), 299–310 (2004)
5. Kumar, A., Bhattacharya, S.: Online Devanagari isolated character recognition for the iPhone using hidden Markov Models. In: International Conference on Students Technology Symposium, pp. 300–304 (2010)
6. Santosh, K.C., Wendlingc, L.: Character recognition based on non-linear multi-projection profiles measure. Int. J. Front. Comput. Sci. **9**(5), 678–690 (2015)
7. Kubatur, S., Sid-Ahmed, M., Ahmadi, M.: A neural network approach to online Devanagari handwritten character recognition. In: International Conference on High Performance Computing and Simulation (2012). https://doi.org/10.1109/HPCSim.2012.6266913

8. Farha, M., Srinivasa, G., Ashwini, A.J., Hemant, K.: Online handwritten character recognition. Int. J. Comput. Sci. **11**(5), 30–36 (2013)

9. Bag, S., Bhowmick, P., Harit, G.: Recognition of Bengali handwritten characters using skeletal convexity and dynamic programming. In: International Conference on Emerging Application of Information Technology, pp. 265–268 (2011)

10. Roy, R.: Stroke-database design for online handwriting recognition in Bangla. Int. J. Mod. Eng. Res. **2**(4), 2534–2540 (2012)

11. Bhattacharya, U., Gupta, B.K., Parui, S.K.: Direction code based features for recognition of online handwritten characters of Bangla. In: International Conference on Document Analysis and Recognition, pp. 58–62 (2007)

12. Parui, S.K., Guin, K., Bhattacharya, U., Chaudhuri, B.B.: Online handwritten Bangla character recognition using HMM. In: International Conference on Pattern Recognition, pp. 1–4 (2008)

13. Sen, S., Sarkar, R., Roy, K., Hori, N.: Recognize online handwritten Bangla characters using hausdorff distance-based feature. In: Satapathy, S.C., Bhateja, V., Udgata, S.K., Pattnaik, P.K. (eds.) Proceedings of the 5th International Conference on Frontiers in Intelligent Computing: Theory and Applications. AISC, vol. 515, pp. 541–549. Springer, Singapore (2017). https://doi.org/10.1007/978-981-10-3153-3_54

14. Sen, S., Mitra, M., Chowdhury, S., Sarkar, R., Roy, K.: Quad-tree based image segmentation and feature extraction to recognize online handwritten Bangla characters. In: Schwenker, F., Abbas, H.M., El Gayar, N., Trentin, E. (eds.) ANNPR 2016. LNCS (LNAI), vol. 9896, pp. 246–256. Springer, Cham (2016). https://doi.org/10.1007/978-3-319-46182-3_21

15. Mondal, T., Bhattacharya, U., Parui, S.K., Das, K., Mandalapu, D.: On-line handwriting recognition of Indian scripts - the first benchmark. In: International Conference on Frontiers in Handwriting Recognition, pp. 200–205 (2010)

16. Sen, S., Sarkar, R., Roy, K.: A simple and effective technique for online handwritten Bangla character recognition. In: Das, S., Pal, T., Kar, S., Satapathy, S.C., Mandal, J.K. (eds.) Proceedings of the 4th International Conference on Frontiers in Intelligent Computing: Theory and Applications (FICTA) 2015. AISC, vol. 404, pp. 201–209. Springer, New Delhi (2016). https://doi.org/10.1007/978-81-322-2695-6_18

17. Sen, S., Bhattacharyya, A., Das, A., Sarkar, R., Roy, K.: Design of novel feature vector for recognition of online handwritten Bangla basic characters. In: Mandal, J., Satapathy, S., Sanyal, M., Bhateja, V. (eds.) Proceedings of the First International Conference on Intelligent Computing and Communication. Advances in Intelligent Systems and Computing, vol. 458, pp. 485–494. Springer, Singapore (2017). https://doi.org/10.1007/978-981-10-2035-3_50

18. Sen, S., Bhattacharyya, A., Sarkar, R., Roy, K., Doermann, D.: Application of structural and topological features to recognize online handwritten Bangla characters. Trans. Asian Low Res. Lang. Inf. Process. **17**(3), 20 (2018). https://doi.org/10.1145/3178457

19. Bandyopadhyay, A., Chakraborty, B.: Development of online handwriting recognition system: a case study with handwritten Bangla character. In: World Congress on Nature and Biologically Inspired Computing, pp. 514–519 (2009)

20. Sen, S., Shaoo, D., Mitra, M., Sarkar, R., Roy, K.: DFA-based online Bangla character recognition. In: Chandra, P., Giri, D., Li, F., Kar, S., Jana, D.K. (eds.) Information Technology and Applied Mathematics. AISC, vol. 699, pp. 175–183. Springer, Singapore (2019). https://doi.org/10.1007/978-981-10-7590-2_13

An Efficient Multi Lingual Optical Character Recognition System for Indian Languages Through Use of Bharati Script

Chandra Sekhar Vorugunti[1]([⊠]), Srinivasa Chakravarthy[2],
and Viswanath Pulabaigari[1]

[1] Indian Institute of Information Technology-SriCity, Chittoor, India
{chandrasekhar.v,viswanath.p}@iiits.in
[2] Indian Institute of Technology-Madras, Chennai, India
schakra@ee.iitm.ac.in

Abstract. Optical character recognition performs a critical part in interpreting videos and documents. Document specific issues like low image quality, distortions, composite background, noise etc. and language specific issues like cursive connectivity among the characters etc. makes OCR challenging and erroneous for Indian languages. The language specific challenges can be overcome by computing the script-based features and can achieve better accuracy. Computing the script based invariant features and patterns is computationally complex and error prone. In this background, we put forward Bharathi script (www.bharatiscript.com) based OCR system in which the inherent drawbacks of Indian scripts i.e. Hindi, Tamil, Telugu etc. are eliminated. The proposed OCR model has been tested on a synthetic dataset of documents of Bharathi script (in which Hindi scripts are converted to Bharathi script). Thorough experimental analysis with varied levels of noise confirms the promising results of character recognition accuracy of the proposed OCR model which out-performs the state-of-the-art OCR systems for Indian scripts. The proposed model achieves 76.70% with test documents consists of 50% noise and 99.98% with test documents of 0% noise.

Keywords: Optical character recognition · Convolutional neural network · Deep learning · Indic script recognition

1 Introduction

Optical character recognition (OCR) consists of identifying handwritten as well as the printed characters from a digital document, produced by scanning a hardcopy, converting the characters into suitable symbolic code thereby producing an editable document [1, 2, 10, 16, 22]. Variations in the physical characteristics of document images, low-quality of the text, noise make the OCR a challenging task. Due to the efficiency in managing voluminous information, OCR has important applications in postal services, banking, office automatization initiatives [3, 6, 8, 34].

Recent advancements in computing capacity and machine learning techniques results in increasing usage of OCR in a developing country like India. In Roman script

© Springer Nature Singapore Pte Ltd. 2019
S. Sundaram and G. Harit (Eds.): DAR 2018, CCIS 1020, pp. 74–83, 2019.
https://doi.org/10.1007/978-981-13-9361-7_7

which is used to express English and other West European languages, there are only 26 characters. Any word is a string of these isolated symbols. Unlike English, most Indic scripts are *abugida* i.e. writing systems where the vowels are inscribed as diacritics on the consonants and a vowel is not explicitly written when it present next to a consonant in a word.

This sequence of diacritics with consonants is termed a composite character or samyuktakshar. A consonant can combine with both each of the vowels and with other consonants of the writing system to form ligatures. Therefore the glyphs representing vowels and consonants are amalgamated according to complex rules of orthography to form new characters. For this reason, a typical Indic script (with the exception of Tamil) has of the order of 10,000 characters. These features make Indic scripts complex, posing significant challenges to development of language related technologies like OCR [5, 11, 13, 20, 21, 27, 30–32, 35].

The recently proposed Bharati script, a novel unified Indic script that can be used to express most major Indian languages, offers some promise in terms of language technology development. The simplicity of its glyphs and lucid and logical compositionality makes it an ideal candidate for OCR development. Like most Indic characters, a typical Bharati character has a three tier structure (upper, base and lower) (Fig. 1). The three tiers are disconnected and are clearly segmentable in OCR by connected component analysis. Most of the glyphs are simple and can be written, for example, in a single stroke without lifting the hand. The glyphs in the upper level always denote the vowel modifier; this level is empty if there is no vowel modifier and the implicit vowel is 'a.' The base (or middle) level always denotes the main consonant. The lower level has diacritics that modify the main consonant present in the base level. For example, of the base level has consonant 'ta', addition of a certain lower level glyph may convert the consonant 'ta' to 'da'. A single Bharati character can have only a single consonant and a vowel. Composite characters, of the type, say, CCV, are expressed as two Bharati characters: first character = C + < halant > ; second character = CV. By virtue of this simplifying feature the number of characters in Bharati script are much smaller than in current Indic script. In fact, using only about 40 glyphs, all the Bharati characters can be composed, which in turn can be used to express the tens of thousands of characters of various Indic scripts.

In this paper we present an OCR system for recognizing Bharati characters. As depicted Fig. 1, the advantage of this system is that it can serve as a common OCR for most major Indian languages since Bharati can be used as a common script to express them. By designing Bharati characters as an additional font (the *NavBharati* fonts) for several of the major Indian languages, we can directly convert Indian language documents into Bharati script (Fig. 1)

The proposed OCR system is tested on Hindi document images of expressed in Bharati script. Deep learning methods are used in this OCR system. Individual glyphs located in the three tiers of Bharati characters are recognized by three separate Convolutional Neural Networks (CNNs). Outputs of the three CNNs are combined using a set of rules thereby converting the original document image into Unicode. The proposed system yields close to 100% performance on noise-free documents.

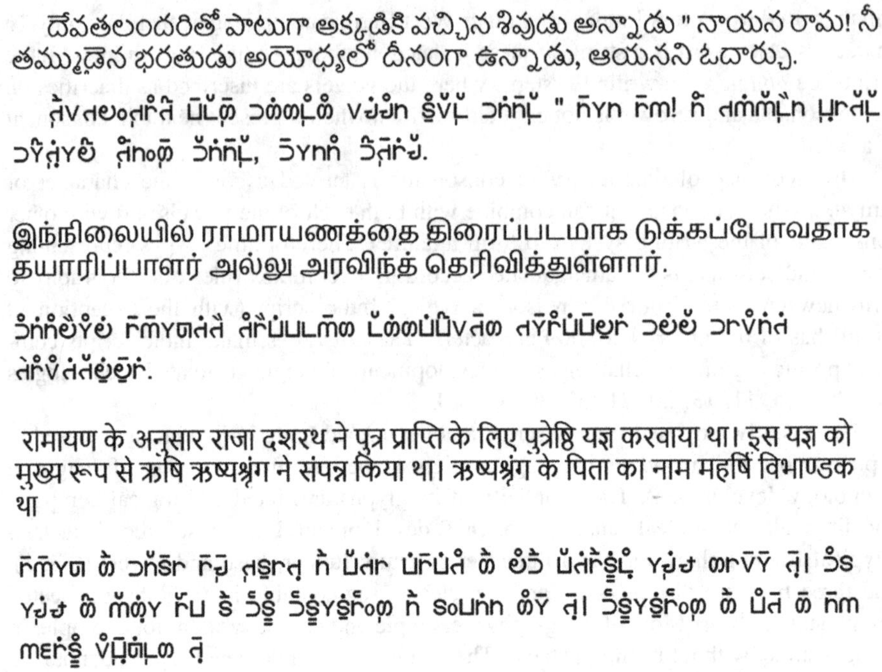

దేవతలందరితో పాటుగా అక్కడికి వచ్చిన శివుడు అన్నాడు " నాయన రామ! నీ తమ్ముడైన భరతుడు అయోధ్యలో దీనంగా ఉన్నాడు, ఆయనని ఓదార్పు.

ನ̃Vⴷలంⴷగⴷ̃ బై̃ⴰ ⴰ౦౦ౖ౦ vⴺⴰౄ ౨౦ౖ ⴰ౦ᅏౖ " ᅏYn ᅐm! ᅌ̃ ⴷᅒᅒ౦ౖᅉ ṵrⴷౖ ⴰYౄᲘౄ ᲘinᲘ ⴰ౦ᅐౖ, ⴰYnᲘ ⴰᲘ̃ⴲ.

இந்நிலையில் ராமாயணத்தை திரைப்படமாக டுக்கப்போவதாக தயாரிப்பாளர் அல்லு அரவிந்த் தெரிவித்துள்ளார்.

ⴰᲘᲘⴺΎⴺ ᅐᅒYⴷⴷ̃ ⴷᲘౄⴰⴷᅒⴰ ᅍ౦౦ౄᅒvⴷⴰ ⴷYᅐౄⴰᲘⴰౖ ⴰⴺⴺ ⴰⴰᲘᲘ ⴷᅒᲘⴷⴷⴲⴺᅐ.

रामायण के अनुसार राजा दशरथ ने पुत्र प्राप्ति के लिए पुत्रेष्टि यज्ञ करवाया था। इस यज्ञ को मुख्य रूप से ऋषि ऋष्यश्रृंग ने संपन्न किया था। ऋष्यश्रृंग के पिता का नाम महर्षि विभाण्डक था

ᅐᅒYⴲ ⴰ̃ ⴰᅌᅐᅐ ᅐⴴ ⴷⴲrⴷ ᅌ̃ ᵽⴷᅐ ᵽᅐᵽ౭ ⴰ̃ ⴺᲘⴰ ᵽⴷᅐⴲౖ Yⴴⴴ ஂⴰᅖᲘ ⴷ̃। ⴰs Yⴴⴴ ⴰ̃ ᅒ౦ᲘY ᅐⴰ ⴲ ⴰⴲ ⴰⴲYⴲᅐᅐ౦ω ᅌ̃ soⴰᅒ౦ ⴰ̃Y ⴷ̃। ⴰⴲYⴲᅐᅐ౦ω ⴰ̃ ᵽⴲ ⴰ̃ ᅐᅒ mⴻᅐⴲ vⴲⴺᅒⴷω ⴷ̃

Fig. 1. The representation of Telugu, Tamil and Hindi text in Bharati script.

2 Related Work

Earliest OCR systems in Hindi/Devnagari can be traced back to the '90s. The first of such models was proposed by Pal et al. [14]. In their Devanagri OCR model, the structural, template features are retrieved from the documents, and a tree classifier is used to recognize the characters and achieved 95.19% recognition accuracy. Subsequently, other models have been proposed which are based on Center Distance Based features, Cut based features, Neighborhood counts based features [15–20]. Chaudhuri et al. [9] proposed the Hindi OCR models based on fuzzy multi-layer perceptron (FMLP), fuzzy Markov random fields (FMRF) and fuzzy support vector machines (FSVM) and achieved significant recognition accuracies 92%.

Models have been proposed based on Gaussian Mixture Models for OCR in Telugu [14], Malayalam, Gujarati and Hindi; these models surpass the traditional models based on SVM [5] on critical metrics like F-Score, recall, precision. Recently Parui et al. [4], Mahmoud et al. [6], Amin et al. [23], Kundu et al. [24], have proposed Indic OCR models adopting Markov models of first and second orders, and Hidden Markov Models (HMM). These models used network parameters derived using statistical techniques as feature values and achieved respectable accuracy of 80.2%, 98.21%, 81% and 85% respectively in Hindi OCR. However, the OCR models based on HMM or the Markov models suffer from the inherent drawback of the requirement of a large number of training samples.

More recently, application of deep learning-based approaches to Indic OCR have pushed up recognition accuracies considerably. [1, 3, 13, 15, 18, 19]. Rohit et al. [15] proposed an LSTM with a delay, for mutual learning of language models and error patterns and shown that their proposed model is strong at detecting errors in Indic OCR with the recognition accuracies of 93.6%.

Recently notable work has been proposed for Indic OCR in the literature. Deep Neural Network (DNN) based models such as Denoising auto-encoders [29], LSTM based models [15, 25, 34], multi-column CNN based models [3, 18, 25, 26, 28], BLSTM based memory networks [7, 26] have been proposed for the recognition of handwritten or printed characters and digits. Ray et al. [26] proposed an OCR model for Oriya language using deep Bidirectional Long Short Term Memory (BLSTM) based Recurrent Neural Network and achieves 4.18% CER and 12.11% WER. In 2018, Shuai et al. [36] proposed an Indic OCR model for documents with low resolution. LSTM and RNN models are used to perform segmentation and retrieval of plurality of text lines from the document images. Recently, Ankan et al. [37], proposed an innovative method which employed fusion techniques that comprises deriving of global and local features from image patches using CNN-LSTM framework and weighting them dynamically for character recognition and achieved 96% accuracy.

3 Proposed Work

As discussed above, the Bharathi characters have the intrinsic advantage of a clear separation among the upper, the base and the lower segments, a simplifying feature absent in other Indic scripts like for example Devanagari. In Devanagari, both vowel and consonant modifiers are connected to the main consonant following complex rules of ligature, a feature that poses significant challenges for OCR in Devanagari.

In this work, we propose an OCR system for Hindi documents expressed in Bharati script. The remaining of the paper is structured as follows: Sect. 3.1 presents our CNN based model architecture. Thorough experimental analysis of our proposed model and comparison with recently proposed models are presented in Sect. 4. Finally, in Sect. 5, we conclude the paper with a defined future direction.

3.1 Proposed CNN Architecture for OCR

In this segment, we do a thorough explanation of the proposed OCR-CNN architecture, preprocessing and data augmentation techniques used for Bharathi OCR.

CNN Architecture
Deep Convolutional Neural Networks (CNN) are multilayer neural networks consists of several convolutional layers interleaved by pooling layers, which down sample the images before feeding to subsequent layers. We used Rectified Linear Units (ReLU) as the activation function in all the convolutional and fully connected layers. To adjust and optimize the weights of the model during backpropagation, the Gradient descent is used and a differentiable loss function is chosen. We have chosen 'adam' as an

optimizer. Apart from the convolution layers, dropouts and pooling layers are added to augment the performance of the model.

The Table 1, depicts our model for training 'Base' segments of Bhrathi character. The first convolutional layer filter the 28×28 input image with 128 kernels of size 3×3 with a padding of 1 pixels. Padding is essential in order to convolve the filter from the very first pixel of the input image. The second convolutional layer takes as input the (zero center normalization and pooled) output of the first convolutional layer and filters it with 128 kernels of size 3×3 with a padding of 1 pixels. The third layer is a max pooling layer has pool size 2×2 and stride of two. Stride indicates the number of steps to be skipped for the next convolution and pooling operations. A dropout of 25% is applied in the max-pooling layer. The first fully connected layer has 128 neurons, whereas the second fully connected layer has 11/17/8 neurons depends the type of the character trained i.e. upper, base or lower. A drop out of 50% is applied to the second fully connected layer. The weights are randomly initialized and the biases equal to zero. We trained the model using Adam for 20 epochs. Our entire framework is implemented using MATLAB deep learning libraries. The training was done using a GeForce GTX 1070 and a TITAN X Pascal GPU, and it took approximately 3 h to run each CNN.

Table 1. Overview of the proposed CNN model architecture.

Layer	Size	Parameters
Convolution + ReLu	$128 \times 3 \times 3$	Pad = 1
Convolution + ReLu	$128 \times 3 \times 3$	Pad = 1
Pooling + Dropout		stride = 2, 0.25
Fully Connected + ReLu + Dropout	128	128, 0.50
Fully Connected	8	

Preprocessing

Since Bharathi script is a novel script, no commercial datasets for Bharathi characters are readily available. Therefore, we developed our own synthetic Bharathi character dataset. As discussed above, Bharathi character is divided into three independent segments 'upper', 'base', 'lower'. There are totally 11 upper, 17 base and 8 lower glyphs in Bharati system.

In line with the restriction on the size of the input images for batch training a convolutional neural network, we resize all the images (upper, base, lower) to a fixed size of 28×28. Afterwards, we convert the training images to gray scale images so that the background pixels have 0 values

Data Augmentation

To deal with the deficiency of sufficient training data for Bharathi script, we augmented each train image by translation through all the eight directions like horizontal, vertical, diagonal, etc. Also, to study the impact of noise on character recognition, we expanded the data set by adding gaussian and the salt and pepper noise.

4   Experiments

Our model consists of three CNNs corresponding to upper, base and lower segments of Bharathi character (Table 1). During training phase of our model, we train each of the three CNN using our synthetic dataset which consists of 6400 images, each of size 28×28 for each Bharathi component (pertaining to upper, base and lower segments). Bharathi character set consists of 11 upper, 17 base and 8 lower characters. Therefore a total $281600 = 6400 * 44$ images are available in the dataset, out of which 4000 were used for training and 2400 were used for validation of each of the upper, base and lower segments. To test the proposed CNN based OCR model, we used test image documents consists of Bharathi characters as shown in appendix. During testing, each Bharathi character is extracted from the input test document, by segmenting the document image first into individual lines, and the lines into individual words and characters respectively. To segment a line, the position (x, y), where the sum of row wise pixel value not equal to zero to the point where the sum is equal to zero is considered. To segment a word from a line, the position from which the column wise sum of pixel values equal to non-zero to the point where it is zero is considered. Similarly, by changing the threshold, we segmented the character from a word. Further, the extracted Bharathi character is split into upper, base and lower segments. In Bharathi, the base segment is mandatory, while the upper and lower segments are optional. Each extracted segment is given as input to the corresponding CNN and the classification result is noted.

4.1   Experimental Protocol

We tested the model performance in OCR with increasing levels of noise ranging from 0% (no noise), 5%, 10%, 20%, 30%, 40%, 50% noise levels added to the character images. We trained the model with images consists of 0% and 2% noise.

In line with the literature, to evaluate our proposed OCR model and compare it with the recent proposed models, we use the standard evaluation metrics i.e. Character Error Rate (CER) and Word Error Rate (WER).

CER and WER are described as (CT: classified text and GT: ground truth text in the below equation)-

$$\text{CER} = \frac{\sum EditDistance(CT, GT)}{\#of\ unicodes\ in\ the\ document} \tag{1}$$

$$\text{WER} = \frac{\sum EditDistance(CT, GT)}{\#of\ words\ in\ the\ document} \tag{2}$$

i.e. the sum of substitutions, deletions and insertions in terms of unicodes essential to convert CT to GT, divided by the amount of unicodes in the ground truth (input test file). WER is defined as the average count of words incorrectly classified.

Note that although Bharati script does not have a separate Unicode, since Bharati characters are an alternative system of expression for Indic languages, the output of the Bharati document in the current case can be expressed in Unicode. As illustrated in

Table 2, our proposed model classification error with 50% of noise in the test document is much less compared to classification error of other models with 0% of noise in the test document. The model proposed by Chaudhuri et al. [9] is recorded less CER compared to our model. The CER value of the model proposed by Chaudhuri et al. [9] is 0.2 at 0% of noise, whereas CER of our proposed model is 0 and 0.33 at 0% and 50% of noise in the test document respectively.

Table 2. Performance evaluation of the proposed model with the recently proposed models in the literature.

Author	WER (%) (Noise–0%)	CER (%) (Noise–0%)
Verma et al. [1]	–	15
Hanmandlu et al. [2]	–	9.35
Rojatkar et al. [3]	–	2.38
Parui et al. [4]	–	17.11
Gyanendra et al. [5]	–	10
Arora et al. [8]	–	7.2
Chaudhuri et al. [9]	–	0.2
Deshpande et al. [10]	–	18
Sharma et al. [11]	–	19.64
Deepti et al. [12]	–	8.6
Sarkhel et al. [13]	–	4.82
Pal et al. [14]	–	4.81
Rohit [15]	–	7.09
Kartik et al. [18]	4.62	2.67
Kartik et al. [18]	11.89	4.9
Kartik et al. [18]	14.09	5.53
Bappaditya et al. [19]	–	3.91
Ritesh et al. [20]	–	4.58
Shrawan et al. [33]	–	3.10
Ray et al. [26]	12.11	4.18
Proposed Model at Noise 50%	1.6	0.33
Proposed Model at Noise 0%	0.002673	0.013674001

Based on these experimental analyses we can confirm that the proposed method of converting the Devanagari/Hindi script to Bhrathi script and performing the OCR using CNN model trained on Bharathi script is yielding results that are far superior to those reported in the literature.

5 Conclusion

In this paper, we have proposed an efficient OCR model based on Convolutional Neural Networks (CNN) for Hindi documents expressed in Bharathi script. That is, instead of the native Devanagari script, and Hindi documents are expressed in Bharati script. The OCR system applied to the Bharati-Hindi document images yielded significantly better performance on the original Devanagari documents. Due to underlying representational power of Bharathi character, unlike its predecessors for OCR, our model achieves excellent classification results. To demonstrate the advantage, we have conducted thorough experiments on the synthetic dataset. The experiments demonstrate a high level of accuracy in character recognition. Furthermore, the proposed model is tested against the test document images upto 50% noise and the recognition results of our model surpassed the state-of-the-art results. Our future work in this direction is to emphasis on the development of more enriched OCR models and large datasets for all the Indian languages.

References

1. Verma, B.K.: Handwritten Hindi character recognition using multilayer perception and radial basis function neural networks. In: IEEE International Conference on Neural Networks, Perth, Australia, pp. 2111–2115 (1995)
2. Hanmandlu, M., Murthy, O.V.R., Madasu, V.K.: Fuzzy model based recognition of handwritten Hindi characters. In: Biennial Conference of the Australian Pattern Recognition Society on Digital Image Computing Techniques and Applications, Glenelg, Australia, pp. 454–461 (2007)
3. Rojatkar, D.V., Chinchkhede, K.D., Sarate, G.G.: Handwritten Devnagari consonants recognition using MLPNN with fivefold cross validation. In: International Conference on Circuits, Power and Computing Technologies (ICCPCT), Nagercoil, India, pp. 1222–1226 (2013)
4. Parui, S.K., Shaw, B.: Offline handwritten Devanagari word recognition: an HMM based approach. In: Ghosh, A., De, R.K., Pal, S.K. (eds.) PReMI 2007. LNCS, vol. 4815, pp. 528–535. Springer, Heidelberg (2007). https://doi.org/10.1007/978-3-540-77046-6_65
5. Verma, G.K., Prasad, S., Kumar, P.: Handwritten Hindi character recognition using curvelet transform. In: Singh, C., Singh Lehal, G., Sengupta, J., Sharma, D.V., Goyal, V. (eds.) ICISIL 2011. CCIS, vol. 139, pp. 224–227. Springer, Heidelberg (2011). https://doi.org/10.1007/978-3-642-19403-0_37
6. Mahmoud, S.: Recognition of writer-independent offline handwritten Arabic (Indian) numerals using hidden Markov models. Sign. Process. **88**(4), 844–857 (2008)
7. Raman, J., Volkmar, F., Jawahar, C.V., Manmatha, R.: BLSTM neural network based word retrieval for Hindi documents. In: International Conference on Document Analysis and Recognition, Beijing, China (2011)
8. Arora, S., Bhattacharjee, D., Nasipuri, M.: Combining multiple feature extraction techniques for handwritten Devnagari character recognition. In: Third International Conference on Industrial and Information Systems, Kharagpur, India, pp. 1–6 (2011)

9. Chaudhuri, A., Mandaviya, K., Badelia, P., Ghosh, S.K.: Optical character recognition systems for Hindi language. Optical Character Recognition Systems for Different Languages with Soft Computing. SFSC, vol. 352, pp. 193–216. Springer, Cham (2017). https://doi.org/10.1007/978-3-319-50252-6_8

10. Deshpande, P.S., Malik, L., Arora, S.: Fine classification and recognition of hand written Devnagari characters with regular expressions and minimum edit distance method. J. Comput. 3(5), 11–17 (2008)

11. Sharma, N., Pal, U., Kimura, F., Pal, S.: Recognition of off-line handwritten Devnagari characters using quadratic classifier. In: Kalra, Prem K., Peleg, S. (eds.) ICVGIP 2006. LNCS, vol. 4338, pp. 805–816. Springer, Heidelberg (2006). https://doi.org/10.1007/11949619_72

12. Khandja, D., Nain, N., Panwara, S.: Hybrid feature extraction algorithm for Devanagari script. ACM Trans. Asian Low Resour. Lang. Inf. Process. 15(1), 2:1–2:10 (2015)

13. Bing, S., Ding, X., Wang, H., Wu, Y.: Discriminative dimensionality reduction for multi-dimensional sequences. IEEE Trans. Pattern Anal. Mach. Intell. 40(1), 77–91 (2018)

14. Pal, U., Wakabayashi, T., Kimura, F.: Comparative study of Devnagari handwritten character recognition using different feature and classifiers. In: International Conference on Document Analysis and Recognition, Barcelona, Spain, July 2009, pp. 1111–1115 (2009)

15. Rohit, S., Devaraj, A., Parag, C., Ganesh, R., Mark, C.: Error detection and corrections in Indic OCR using LSTMs. In: 14th IAPR International Conference on Document Analysis and Recognition (2017)

16. Parul, S., Sanjay, B.D.: Multilingual character segmentation and recognition schemes for Indian document images. IEEE Access, XX (2017)

17. Jayadevan, R., Satish, R., Kolhe, P.M., Patil, U.P.: Offline recognition of Devanagari script: a survey. IEEE Trans. Syst. Man. Cybern. 41, 782–796 (2011)

18. Dutta, K., Krishnan, P., Mathew, M., Jawahar, C.V.: Towards accurate handwritten word recognition for Hindi and Bangla. In: Rameshan, R., Arora, C., Dutta Roy, S. (eds.) NCVPRIPG 2017. CCIS, vol. 841, pp. 470–480. Springer, Singapore (2018). https://doi.org/10.1007/978-981-13-0020-2_41

19. Bappaditya, C., Bikash, S., Jayanta, A., Ujjwal, B., Swapan, K.P.: Does deeper network lead to better accuracy: a case study on handwritten Devanagari characters. In: 13th IAPR International Workshop on Document Analysis Systems (DAS) (2018)

20. Ritesh, S., Nibaran, D., Aritra, D., Mahantapas, K., Mita, N.: A multi-scale deep quad tree based feature extraction method for the recognition of isolated handwritten characters of popular Indic scripts. Pattern Recogn. 71, 78–93 (2017)

21. Ukil, S., Ghosh, S., Md Obaidullah, S.M., Santosh, K.C., Roy, K., Das, N.: Deep learning for word-level handwritten Indic script identification. arxiv 2018 (2018)

22. Sankaran, N., Jawahar, C.: Error detection in highly inflectional languages in document analysis and recognition. In: 12th International Conference on (ICDAR), pp. 1135–1139 (2013)

23. Amin, A.: Off-line Arabic character recognition. Pattern Recognit. 31(5), 517–530 (1998)

24. Kundu, A., He, Y., Bahl, P.: Recognition of handwritten word: first and second order hidden Markov model based approach. In: Proceedings of the Computer Society Conference on Computer Vision and Pattern Recognition, CVPR 1988, pp. 457–462 (1988)

25. Ul-Hasan, A., Bin Ahmed, S., Rashid, F., Shafait, F., Breuel, T.M.: Online printed Urdu Nastaleeq script recognition with bidirectional LSTM networks. In: 2013 12th International Conference on Document Analysis and Recognition, pp. 1061–1065 (2013)

26. Ray, A., Rajeswar, S., Chaudhury, S.: Text recognition using deep BLSTM networks. In: 2015 Eighth International Conference on Advances in Pattern Recognition (ICAPR), pp. 1–6 (2015)

27. Roy, S., Das, N., Kundu, M., Nasipuri, M.: Handwritten isolated Bangla compound character recognition: a new benchmark using a novel deep learning approach. Pattern Recognit. Lett. **90**, 15–21 (2017)
28. Ciresan, D., Meier, U.: Multi-column deep neural networks for online handwritten Chinese character classification. In: International Joint Conference on Neural Networks (IJCNN), pp. 1–6 (2015)
29. Pal, A., Pawar, J.D.: Recognition of online handwritten Bangla characters using hierarchical system with denoising autoencoders. In: International Conference on Computation of Power, Energy Information and Communication (ICCPEIC) 2015, pp. 47–51 (2015)
30. Pal, A.: Bengali handwritten numeric character recognition using denoising autoencoders. In: 2015 IEEE International Conference on Engineering and Technology (ICETECH), pp. 1–6 (2015)
31. Saikat, R., Nibaran, D., Mahantapas, K., Mita, N.: Handwritten isolated Banga compound character recognition: a new benchmark using a novel deep learning approach. Pattern Recogn. Lett. **90**, 15–21 (2017)
32. Rahul, P., Soumen, B.: Shape decomposition-based handwritten compound character recognition for Bangla OCR. J. Vis. Commun. Image Represent. **50**, 123–134 (2018)
33. Shrawan, R., Shloak, G., Basant, A.: Devanagri character recognition model using deep convolution neural network. J. Stat. Manag. Syst. **21**(4), 593–599 (2018)
34. Ankan, K.B., Aishik, K., Ayan, K.B., Abir, B., Partha, P.R., Umapada, P.: Script identification in natural scene image and video frames using an attention based convolutional-LSTM network. Pattern Recogn. **85**, 172–184 (2019)
35. Meduri, A., Navneet, G.: Optical character recognition for sanskrit using convolution neural networks. In: 13th IAPR International Workshop on Document Analysis Systems (2018)
36. Shuai, W., Maneesh, K.S.: Systems and methods for optical character recognition for low-resolution Documents. Patent: US20180101726A1 (2018)
37. Ankan, K.B., Aishik, K., Abir, B., Partha, P.R., Umapada, P.: Script identification in natural scene image and video frames using an attention based convolutional-LSTM network. Elsevier J. Pattern Recogn. **85**, 172–184 (2019)

Character and Word Segmentation

Telugu Word Segmentation
Using Fringe Maps

Koteswara Rao Devarapalli[1,2(✉)] and Atul Negi[2]

[1] Department of Computer Science and Engineering,
Mahatma Gandhi Institute of Technology, Hyderabad 500075, India
dkrao@mgit.ac.in

[2] School of Computer and Information Sciences, University of Hyderabad,
Gachibowli, Hyderabad 500046, India
atulcs@uohyd.ernet.in

Abstract. In this paper, we propose a word segmentation method that is based on fringe maps on Telugu script. Our objective is to create a data set of word images for enabling direct training for recognition on those. The standard methods employed for the task of word segmentation in Telugu OCR systems are projection profiles and run-length smearing. However those methods have their limitations. In this work a different application of fringe maps is shown for line segmentation into words. Fringes were previously applied successfully for carrying out classification and line segmentation. Telugu script, which has consonant modifiers that are usually placed below or below-right to the base consonants. This kind of orthographic property leads to characters that may touch each other. One way to deal with touched characters is to make use of segmentation free methods, which do not need prior segmentation of word images into characters or connected components. The novelty of our method is that we analyze fringe maps of document images to find an appropriate fringe value threshold and apply it for word segmentation of Telugu documents. Encouraging results are observed with our fringe value threshold based word segmentation. We observe that choosing higher threshold fringe values leads to under-segmentation of words, whereas lower values cause over-segmentation of words. Our word segmentation approach is successfully compared with the widely used projection profiles based word segmentation method.

Keywords: Akshara · Fringe distance · Telugu OCR ·
Word segmentation

1 Introduction

The current trend in Telugu optical character recognition (OCR) is that deep neural networks have been successfully demonstrated for improving the performance of existing systems. Compared to the traditional recognition approaches, deep learning frameworks demand significantly large training sets for effective

© Springer Nature Singapore Pte Ltd. 2019
S. Sundaram and G. Harit (Eds.): DAR 2018, CCIS 1020, pp. 87–96, 2019.
https://doi.org/10.1007/978-981-13-9361-7_8

modeling. Now a significant percentage of efforts is required to prepare such training data.

The standard training data sets are not available in sufficient magnitude to develop robust, end-to-end Telugu OCR systems based on deep architectures [1]. Previous methods rely on either own data sets [7] or the standard corpus of 5000 document images scanned from the popular old books as the part of a consortium project. Due to practical difficulties of clarity of the images [6] cited results only on 1000 pages. Few authors prepared synthetic data sets and made them public for the research needs. Broken and touched characters are the major problems that can effect the performance of Telugu OCR systems. In our work we do not rely on segmentation of connected components or characters [2,10], but we segment words using fringe distance method. The goal of avoiding character segmentation is to prepare data set of words for enabling the recognition of broken and touching characters.

1.1   Properties of Telugu Orthography

Telugu has its own phonetic script, with well rounded *aksharas* (characters). Telugu text is composed of *aksharas*, which are the basic units of orthography and are made up of rounded curves. Telugu script consists of glyphs for basic vowels, basic consonants, vowel modifiers and consonant modifiers.

In Telugu script, there are 15 vowels and 35 consonants. It has corresponding vowel modifiers and consonant modifiers. Unlike Roman script, Telugu syllables have a direct correspondence to their orthographic units [8]. Vowel modifiers are placed at the top portions of the basic glyphs, whereas the consonant modifiers are found below or below-right places of the symbols. These modifiers and printing methods may cause broken and touched characters. The prevailing issues in Telugu character recognition are mainly due to broken and touched characters. The widely used conventional connected component based methods may fail due to the segmentation errors that may occur because of the broken and touched characters. In the following sections of the paper, the related work is reported in Sect. 2 and we describe our word segmentation approach in Sect. 3. The data preparation task is explained in Sect. 4, and finally the conclusion is made in Sect. 5.

2   Related Work

Our work mainly consists of data preparation through applying a novel fringe distance method to perform line and word segmentations. We avoid segmentation of either connected components or characters, because character level segmentation may cause broken and touched characters.

Fringe distance method involves generation of fringe map for a given binary document image. A fringe map is the function of fringe distance represented as numeric value per pixel, which is incremented on each move away from a foreground pixel. The concept of fringe distance to generate fringe maps of characters is first employed for demonstrating character recognition [3]. It is also applied successfully for Telugu character recognition [8]. Consecutive Telugu text lines may overlap at few of the symbol positions due to some of the font types and glyphs for vowel modifiers and consonant modifiers. The standard methods of line segmentation such as horizontal projection, and run length smearing may fail and can cause segmentation error. The peak fringe number (PFN) concept is used to segment lines of Telugu document images with some overlap between them due to modifiers [4]. They segment lines of a document depending on fringe map creation, retaining peak fringe numbers between consecutive black pixels per each column, and filtering unwanted fringe numbers that occur inside characters.

In the recent work on Telugu character recognition [1], they prepared a synthetic data set for training Convolutional neural network classifier, which does not need any explicit feature extraction. It relies on connected component extraction, which causes segmentation errors. *Indic* scripts have got unique orthographic properties due to the existence of separate glyphs for vowel and consonant modifiers. One of the orthographic properties of Telugu script is that consonant modifiers are spatially spread across the middle and lower zones. The concept of peak fringe numbers (PFNs) is used for finding zones and to define a first level classifier before training models [9]. In their work, peak fringe numbers that occur due to white space inside characters is used for identifying middle line across characters. They employ the middle line as the reference in finding zones, which enable grouping of words into words with consonant modifiers and without consonant modifiers. This kind of grouping is aimed for effective character modeling. For word segmentation, a novel fringe distance based method is employed. Fringe maps of given binary document images can be computed using fringe distance method, which is previously used for classification [3], feature extraction [8] and line segmentation [4].

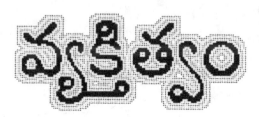

Fig. 1. Example fringe map of a word image pattern is shown. Fringe numbers are colored as 0-Blue, 1-Cyan, 2-Red, 3-Cyan, and 4-Magenta respectively. (Color figure online)

3   Word Segmentation

Projection profiles based word segmentation algorithm makes use of zeros in the projection that defines segmentation points. Run-length smearing algorithm (RLSA) can be used to perform marking in horizontal direction on the complement of input binary image for finding the segmentation points. In RLSA, we change adjacent 0's to 1's if their count is less than or equal to a threshold to make smearing.

In this paper, we use the fringe maps of document images to attempt the word segmentation task for Telugu OCR. A fringe map gives various levels of the fringe (background) of a pattern. Different levels can be used for different segmentation needs such as line segmentation, word segmentation and character segmentation. Fringe map of an example word image is shown in Fig. 1.

3.1   Fringe Map

Fringes may be thought of as a kind of distance transform on background pixels in the image. Binarized text images are used for creating fringe maps of document images. Fringe map of a binary image can be computed through finding fringe distances. For an image, fringe distance of a pixel can be defined as the pixel distance to the closest foreground pixel. Fringe map was introduced for character recognition [3] and first used for Telugu OCR [8]. Towards improving Telugu OCR system, fringe maps were used for line segmentation [4] and for finding modifier zones of word images to enable classification of them into major classes such as words having modifiers and words having no modifiers [9].

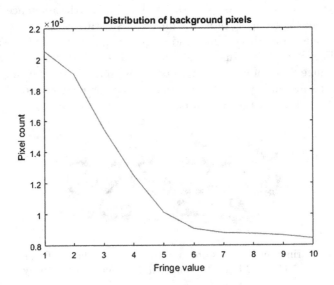

Fig. 2. Distribution of fringe values of a document image. The higher pixel counts are due to fringe values such as 1, and 2. Whereas lower counts are due to fringes that occur as we move away from the foreground text.

The first step in fringe map creation is to assign 0 and -1 fringe values to every black and white pixels respectively. Then we look for white pixels in the horizontal, vertical, and diagonal directions of every black pixel and are set to the

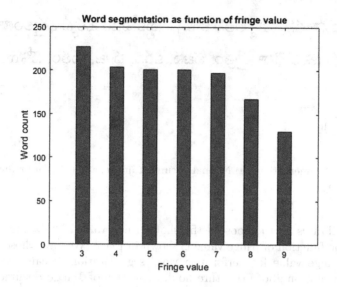

Fig. 3. Word count statistics for an example document image, over-segmentation of words is observed for the fringe values less than or equal to 3, whereas under-segmentation is found for the fringe values greater than or equal to 6.

fringe 1. Further pixels with fringe value 1 are followed to label their neighbors having −1 with fringe 2. This numbering is continued until there are no pixels with number −1. Thus, for each input document image, we compute its fringe map.

3.2 Fringe Value Thresholding Algorithm

The goal of this work is to segment word regions from document images for Telugu OCR. We use the standard preprocessing methods such as Otsu's binarization to convert Gray scale images into binary ones and median filter with 3×3 kernel to remove commonly occurring noise. The proposed Telugu word segmentation involves different tasks on input document images. Input data to our word segmentation method can be either document images or line images. The main tasks involved are creating fringe map, filtering unwanted fringe values, filtering smaller undesirable connected components, locating word regions, finding segmentation points, and extracting word images. Fringe maps were used [3] for character recognition. The novelty of our work is that fringe maps are filtered based on a fringe value threshold, which is chosen empirically to facilitate the finding of word segmentation points.

We analyze the distribution of fringe values of different document images. Distribution of fringes for a document image is shown in Fig. 2. The higher pixel counts are due to fringe values such as 1, and 2. Whereas lower counts are due to fringes that occur as we move away from the foreground text. The purpose this analysis is to know the distribution of background pixels around foreground

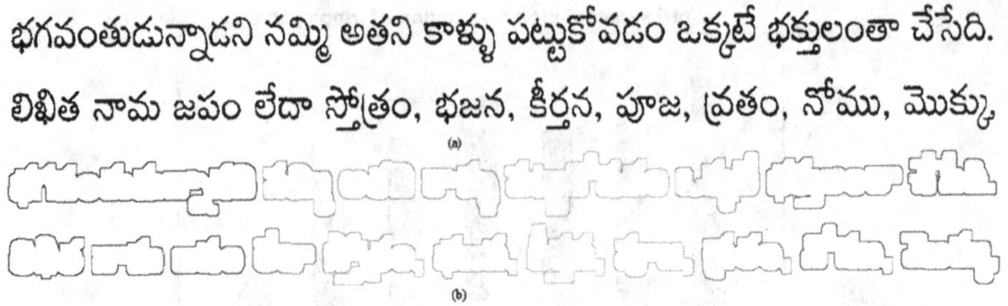

భగవంతుడున్నాడని నమ్మి అతని కాళ్ళు పట్టుకోవడం ఒక్కటే భక్తులంతా చేసేది.

లిఖిత నామ జపం లేదా స్తోత్రం, భజన, కీర్తన, పూజ, వ్రతం, నోము, మొక్కు

(a)

(b)

Fig. 4. Word Segmentation: (a) Normal document image, and (b) Word regions having fringe value 5.

text. It facilitates us to choose a threshold fringe value. The segmentation of words as the function of fringe value is shown in Fig. 3. We have chosen 5 as the threshold fringe value for performing word segmentation, because we observe under-segmentation above this threshold. A portion of Telugu document image and corresponding labeled word regions using fringe value threshold 5 is shown in Fig. 4. For a range of 1–10 fringe values, we have empirically observed the distribution of fringes around the text. Towards the task of filtering unwanted fringes, we have chosen fringe value 5 as the threshold(th1). Filtering involves keeping the pixels with threshold and setting values of all other pixels to zero. We also filter out smaller undesirable connected components, which are having

---

Algorithm 1. Word Segmentation

1: **procedure** WORDSEGMENTATION(*DocImage*)   ▷ DocImage or line image
2:     **for all** *whitePixels* **do**   ▷ Create fringe map
3:         *whitePixel* ← −1
4:     **end for**
5:     **for all** *blackPixels* **do**
6:         *whiteNeighborsOfblackPixel* ← 1
7:     **end for**
8:     *label* ← 1
9:     **repeat**
10:        **for all** *Pixels with label* **do**
11:            *label* ← *label* + 1
12:            *whiteNeighborsOfPixels* ← *label*
13:        **end for**
14:    **until** *all whitePixels are labeled*
                                                        ▷ Find word regions
15:    Filter unwanted fringe values using a threshold *th*1
16:    Filter unwanted smaller components having pixels less than a threshold *th*2
17:    Locate word regions
18:    Find segmentation points
19:    Extract word images
20: **end procedure**

Table 1. Performance of different word segmentation approaches for the segmentation of Telugu word images

Book	Pages	Text-words	Algorithm	Word-imgs	Errors
DiavamVaipu	122	21775	Fringe value thresholding	21832	57
			Projection profiles	21788	13
7-different books	30	5625	Fringe value thresholding	5622	15
			Projection profiles	5629	4

a count of pixels less than a threshold(th2), the value of th2 is 100. The goal of this task is to find the background regions around the words of text and these regions helps us to determine the segmentation points. The extraction of words is carried out relying on segmentation points. We compare our method with the widely used projection profiles based word segmentation approach. The results are given in Table 1. The projection profiles based approach causes over-segmentation when there is more gap between characters of words. The merit of this approach is that it can be applied on either document images or line images. We observe that higher threshold fringe values cause under-segmentation (merged words) shown in Fig. 5, whereas lower values lead to over-segmentation (split words). In this paper, we directly applied fringe value thresholding on document images. When there is no significant gap between lines, our method requires to execute on line images for extracting word images.

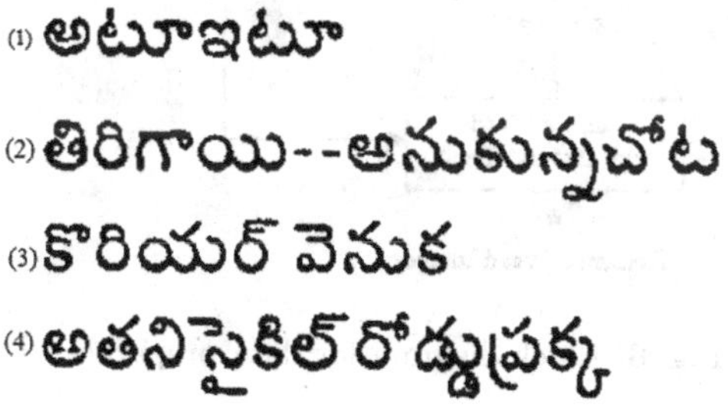

Fig. 5. Four cases are shown, each case has multiple words, which are segmented as single word due to merging of words.

4   Data Preparation

Data preparation involves segmentation of words from both standard corpus of document images and synthetic documents. Our Telugu standard corpus consists of around 5000 document images of 26 Telugu books printed in different font type and size combinations. These document images are scanned with 300 dots per inch (DPI) from old popular books and the corresponding ground truth is created as part of the consortium projects.

Corpus also consists of degraded documents due to aging and poor print quality. In the previous works [5,6] 1000 document images of the standard corpus are used as the common bench mark data set. Further, we include some synthetic document images created using recently released Telugu Unicode fonts. The synthetic documents are scanned in different DPIs such as 200, 250 and 300. Deep learning methods can automatically learn features from the raw data and enable developing recognition systems with no explicit feature extraction. But, implicit learning features demands a lot of training data, particularly for the problems involving high-dimensional data such as images, videos.

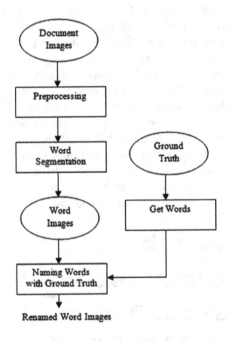

Fig. 6. Block diagram for data preparation.

Data preparation task consumes significant amount of time and can be expensive, especially when real world data is to be included. The recent trend in computer vision is that pre-trained models are available, which can be used to build sophisticated vision models using very little amount of data. Input to our data preparation task is the Telugu document images and their ground truth files. Output is the word images renamed with the corresponding ground truth. The sub-tasks of our data preparation are shown in Fig. 6. Name of each word is composed of numeric codes of the book, line, and word, as well as its ground truth, which is a sequence of Telugu characters written in English script. The benefit of including ground truth in renaming word images is to enable straightforward training without requiring explicit label files. It also facilitates manual, and programmatic checking of the word images and their ground truth for correctness.

. Data preparation involves two main sub-tasks: word segmentation and text processing. The former one consists of preprocessing the Telugu document images followed by segmentation of words. After the word segmentation is accomplished, the later main sub-task is Telugu text processing that involves isolation of ground truth words. For each ground truth text file, it is divided into lines and then words are isolated from lines of text. We rename each word image with its book code, line number, word number and ground truth. This kind of renaming enables easy verification of the word images against their ground truth for correctness.

4.1   Data Augmentation

Data augmentation is a method to increase our training samples to a large amount. Since deep learning methods demand big data for training the models, we apply augmentation methods to increase our word samples that consists of broken and touched characters.

The input to our data augmentation task is the word images extracted from the standard corpus of documents, which are scanned with the efforts of consortium project teams. Our main goal is to improve the Telugu OCR system performance despite the presence of broken and touched characters. We augment them through a number of random transformations, thus our model would never see twice exact the same image. This is to prevent over fitting and better generalize the model. It is particularly useful, when the training data set is small. We employ seven primary data augmentations for our data preparation: rotation, shift, rescale, shear, and zoom. For rotation, it is to rotate images in degrees (0–10), and shift transformation aims to translate images both vertically and horizontally. For rescale, we multiply the data by a value. Shear operation is for applying shearing transformations, whereas zoom is for zooming inside images. Further, fill mode is the strategy used for filling in newly created pixels, which can appear after a rotation or a shift. Thus data augmentation enables us to increase word samples that have a few instances in the corpus.

5   Conclusion

Our work makes use of the concept of fringe distance transform, which is used to generate fringe maps of Telugu document images. The word segmentation is achieved by choosing a threshold fringe value through analyzing the distribution of fringes of document images. The word segmentation is described as the function of fringe value. The merit of this approach is that it can be applied on either document images or line images. We observe that choosing higher fringe values cause under-segmentation of words, whereas lower values lead to over-segmentation of words. In this paper, we directly applied fringe value thresholding on document images. When there is no significant gap between lines, our method requires to execute on line images to extract word images.

The data preparation involves extraction of word images from standard corpus, and then the application of augmentation methods to increase the word samples that involve instances of broken and touching characters. Further, we use Unicode based text processing to obtain ground truth words and rename the word images with their ground truth. Renaming facilitates easy verification of word images and their ground truth for correctness. This kind of data set is to be used for deep learning methods, which require significantly large data sets for better modeling.

References

1. Achanta, R., Hastie, T.: Telugu OCR framework using deep learning. CoRR abs/1509.05962 (2015)
2. Bhagvati, C., Ravi, T., Kumar, S.M., Negi, A.: On developing high accuracy OCR systems for Telugu and other Indian scripts. In: 2002 Proceedings of the Language Engineering Conference, pp. 18–23, December 2002
3. Brown, R.L.: The fringe distance measure: an easily calculated image distance measure with recognition results comparable to Gaussian blurring. IEEE Trans. Syst. Man Cybern. **24**(1), 111–115 (1994)
4. Koppula, V.K., Negi, A.: Fringe map based text line segmentation of printed Telugu document images. In: 2011 International Conference on Document Analysis and Recognition, pp. 1294–1298, September 2011
5. Krishnan, P., Sankaran, N., Singh, A.K., Jawahar, C.V.: Towards a robust OCR system for Indic scripts. In: 2014 11th IAPR International Workshop on Document Analysis Systems (DAS), pp. 141–145, April 2014
6. Kumar, P.P., Bhagvati, C., Negi, A., Agarwal, A., Deekshatulu, B.L.: Towards improving the accuracy of Telugu OCR systems. In: ICDAR, pp. 910–914. IEEE Computer Society (2011)
7. Lakshmi, C.V., Patvardhan, C.: An optical character recognition system for printed Telugu text. Pattern Anal. Appl. **7**(2), 190–204 (2004)
8. Negi, A., Bhagvati, C., Krishna, B.: An OCR system for Telugu. In: ICDAR, pp. 1110–1114. IEEE Computer Society (2001)
9. Rao, D.K., Negi, A.: Orthographic properties based Telugu text recognition using hidden Markov models. In: 2017 14th IAPR International Conference on Document Analysis and Recognition (ICDAR), vol. 05, pp. 45–50, November 2017
10. Vasantha Lakshmi, C., Patvardhan, C.: A multi-font OCR system for printed Telugu text. In: 2002 Proceedings of the Language Engineering Conference, pp. 7–17, December 2002

An Efficient Character Segmentation Algorithm for Connected Handwritten Documents

Vishal Rajput[1], N. Jayanthi[2(✉)], and S. Indu[2]

[1] Department of Electronics and Communication Engineering,
PDPM-Indian Institute of Information Technology,
Design and Manufacturing Jabalpur, Jabalpur 482005, MP, India
vishal.stark42@gmail.com
[2] Department of Electronics and Communication Engineering,
Delhi Technological University, Delhi, India
{njayanthi,s.indu}@dce.ac.in

Abstract. This paper proposes an efficient method of character segmentation for handwritten text. The main challenge in character segmentation of hand-written text is the varied size of each letter in different documents, connected alphabets in a word in cursive writing and the presence of ligatures within an open character. Hence, this paper proposes an adaptive vertical pixel count algorithm to solve the problem of over-segmentation due to the presence of open characters such as 'w', 'v' and 'm'. Proposed algorithm works effectively against both the hand-written and standard text. The proposed method is evaluated on IAM and self-created data set.

Keywords: Optical Character Recognition ·
Potential segmented column

1 Introduction

Since the advent of computers, a whole lot of information has paved its way to the digital format. There are so many digital platforms to save data. Despite the availability of so many digital platforms, paper and pen are still in use. There will always be manuscripts and books which will not be available in the soft copy format. No matter the amount of the digital space, information will still be present in the hard copy format. Since old documents are very fragile and degrades with time so they need a digital storage. Such systems which can interpret handwritten or printed documents needs to build. To solve this problem, researchers use a tool called OCR (Optical Character Recognition). An OCR is a tool which extracts text from images and saves them in a machine-readable format. Today there are types of OCR available in the market but almost each one of them suffers some kind of drawback. Modern day OCR works well on the standard and non-connected text, but they are ineffective for handwritten

© Springer Nature Singapore Pte Ltd. 2019
S. Sundaram and G. Harit (Eds.): DAR 2018, CCIS 1020, pp. 97–105, 2019.
https://doi.org/10.1007/978-981-13-9361-7_9

and connected text. The primary reason for the failure of most of the OCR is the inability to segment the characters present in a word. Because of different writing styles it is very difficult to find the correct segmentation point. Generally, computer finds it difficult to find the correct segmentation point. To solve this issue proposed algorithm should be intelligent enough to adapt to different writing styles.

2   Related Work

In the past, researchers have used different schemes for the character segmentation. Every technique suffers some or the other drawback. Different errors which happens generally during the segmentation are Bad-Segmentation, Over-Segmentation, and Miss-Segmentation. Figure 1 shows all the different types of errors. Some researchers proposed segmentation based on the average width of a character. This approach works only when the characters are of uniform width and fails when the characters present in a word are of non-uniform width. This technique is useless for normal writing sample because of the difference in each character's width.

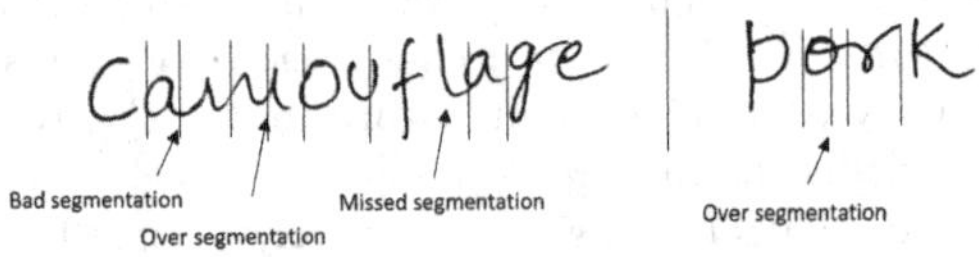

Fig. 1. Images showing types of segmentation errors.

In this paper, an improved version of the vertical pixel count algorithm is presented. The Proposed technique was tested on IAM and self-created data set to check the efficiency of the presented algorithm. The proposed method is simple and very effective on connected text but in case of overlapping characters obtained results are not satisfactory. Further investigation will be made to handle overlapping characters by segmenting at a slope instead of vertical segmentation.

Javed et al. [2] proposed a character segmentation algorithm based on white spaces between characters. This algorithm works fine for standard text but fails for connected text. Javed's algorithm is not able to produce any result in presence of a ligature.

Rehman et al. [7] used an implicit technique to divide the image into very fine parts (much smaller than the words). And then every part passes through a neural network which identifies presence of a character in that part. It is a character identification technique whose by-product is character segmentation [6]. This approach is costly in terms of time it takes to segment the character. Its accuracy is dependent on the number of samples used to train the neural network. Another reason for the failure of their technique is that it often confuses 'w' as 'u' & 'i' or 'u' as 'i' & 'i'.

In [10], a graph model describes the possible locations for segmenting neighbouring characters. Then they use an average longest path algorithm to identify the globally optimal segmentation. This approach may fail when the lexicon domain is insufficient.

Choudhary et al. [1] have used a pixel counting approach for the character segmentation. If words are well separated, proposed method takes the average of all PSC's to solve the problem of over-segmentation. And in case of open characters like 'w', 'u' or 'm' they use the distance between two PSC's, if it is less than 7 following PSC's merges with the previous PSC. A significant problem in their proposed approach is to decide the threshold value i.e. 7 (in their case). Threshold value will change if there is large variation in characters width in a single word. Even with consistent character width same threshold may not work when same word is in large font. Choudhary's technique performs very bad in cases like 'm' & 'n'.

Yamada et al. [12] used multiple segmentation determined by contour analysis for Cursive handwritten word recognition and Saba et al. [9] considered a neural network for cursive character recognition which gives the confidence for the similarity of a given character with all the characters in the database. In [11], a probabilistic model based on Word model recognizer is used to segment the handwritten words. Lee et al. [3] used a totally different technique in which the character segmentation regions are determined by using projection profiles and topographic features extracted from the gray-scale images. A multi-stage graph search algorithm finds a nonlinear character segmentation path in each character which is the basis for the segmentation point.

3   Problem Statement

There are various challenges in the character segmentation of handwritten words due to the varied nature of individual's hand-writing. Most significant problem in character segmentation is the presence of a connected component in a given word. Cursive nature of words adds another layer of difficulty in the segmentation process. Overlapping characters also create lots of problem in segmentation as it increases the chance of a point wrongly identified as a segmentation point. Most of the characters can be written in multiple ways thus a holistic solution is required which is able to identify the correct segmentation point even after all the feature differences in the same character. Proposed method solves the problem of connected components by using the modified vertical pixel count.

4   Proposed Methodology

The proposed method uses local maxima and minima to convert vertical pixel count graph into a binary graph which is the basis for finding the segmentation points in a word. The binarized graph is processed adaptively according to the width of peaks present in it to identify the wrong segmentation points and finally potential segmentation points are marked i.e. positions where a word is segmented.

Characters which doesn't have any type of full or partial loop in them like m, n, u, w, are hard to segment. These characters are often over segmented because of multiple local minima's in vertical pixel count graph as shown in Fig. 1. To avoid the over-segmentation problem, peaks in vertical pixel count graph are combined in an adaptive manner to find the correct PSC (Potentially Segmented Column). In Fig. 2(a), three peaks of character are combined together to find the correct segmentation point. Same is the case in Fig. 2(b), where peaks are combined to solve over segmentation in character 'n'.

In the proposed method vertical pixel count of a word is used as the basis for finding the PSC's. The proposed text segmentation algorithm is summarized by Algorithm 1 and explained in detail in the further subsection.

Algorithm 1
___

1. Image pre-processing for noise removal and contrast enhancement.
2. Formation of vertical pixel count graph.
3. Binarizing the vertical pixel count graph.
4. Assignment of Flag value (either 0 or 1) to each peak according to their width.
5. Merging the peaks to eliminate the wrong segmentation point based on the Flag value of peaks.
6. Centre of each trough of the processed graph is used as the point of segmentation.
7. If a character is segmented at a position where PSC cuts the text more than once, ignore that PSC.

4.1   Formation of Binarized Graph

Given word image is read vertically from top to down following the same along the column (width) of the image. Vertical pixel count graph for the sample word "guys" is shown in Fig. 3(b). It is clear from the sample word graph shown in Fig. 3(b) that the vertical pixel graphs is not uniform in nature. To make further processing easy, obtained vertical pixel count graph is converted into binary

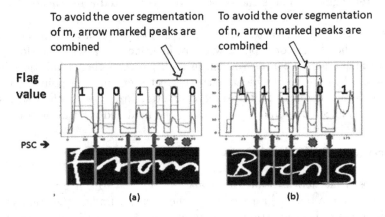

Fig. 2. How peaks are combined in vertical pixel count graph to solve the problem of over segmentation.

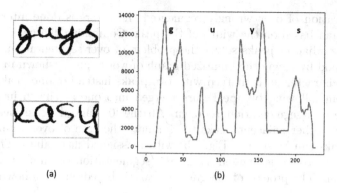

Fig. 3. (a) Sample word "guys" (self-created dataset) and "easy" (from IAM dataset) to show the sample images. (b) Pixel count of word "guys".

graph. The Obtained vertical pixel count graph is converted into a binary graph P_y based on basic thresholding operation mentioned in Eq. 1 and the binarized graph is shown in Fig. 4(a).

$$P_y = \begin{cases} 1, & \text{if } pixel\ count > 10 \\ 0, \text{otherwise} \end{cases} \tag{1}$$

4.2 Assignment of Flag Values to the Peak

To identify the over/wrongly segmented characters, peak's width in the binarized graph needs to be checked. Some peaks are very short in width as compared to the rest of the peaks. Peaks which are having width lesser than the average width indicates an over/wrongly segmented word. Now, to mark the characters which are over/wrongly segmented, the peak of that particular character in the binarized graph P_y is flagged with value '0'. For marking the peaks, comparison of each peak width in the binarized graph P_y is done with the average peak width W_{avg} to assign the flag values to be either 0 or 1 based on the Eqs. 2 and 3. Binarized flagged graph is shown in Fig. 4(a).

$$W_{avg} = \frac{\sum_{i=1}^{n} W_i}{n}, \tag{2}$$

$$F_{ip} = \begin{cases} 0, & \text{if } W_i < k \cdot W_{avg} \\ 1, & \text{otherwise,} \end{cases} \tag{3}$$

where F_{ip} is the flag used for marking of $i_t h$ peak, k is a constant whose value lies between 0.6 & 0.9 and W_i is the width of $i_t h$ peak.

The optimum value of $k = 0.7$ is obtained by experimenting multiple times. Peaks width is compared to $0.7W_{avg}$ because single character width often varies quite largely with the average width.

Identification of over/wrongly segmented characters is done after marking the peaks and based on the width of the peak. Combining the peak flagged as '0' with the adjacent peaks solves the problem of over-segmentation. This can be understood by seeing the binarized graph of word "guys" shown in Fig. 4(a), where the character 'u' is marked with two peaks instead of one peak, to solve this problem following two peaks are merged into one as shown in Fig. 4(b), solving the over-segmentation problem. All the '0' flagged peaks needs to be merged with other adjacent peaks to eliminate the case of over-segmentation. Merged peaks can be seen in Fig. 4(b) with reassigned flag values. The middle point of each trough is marked as an SC (segmentation column), i.e. point of segmentation. The process of merging of peaks is based on the following ways:

- **CASE 1:** If the successive peak/peaks are marked as flag 0 initially, merge them to form a single peak and reassign it as flag 1, removing the over-segmentation.
- **CASE 2:** If peaks adjacent to flag 0 are flag 1 then the distance from both the adjacent peaks is calculated and flag 0 peak is merged to the peak which has a shorter distance from it.

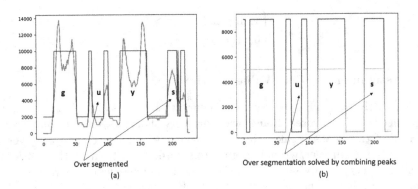

Fig. 4. (a) Pixel count converted into binary graph (b) Smaller peaks merged into one peak (Ti & Pi is width of ith trough & peak respectively).

4.3   Elimination of False PSC's

If the obtained PSC intersects the text more than once (Fig. 5(a) 'o' is over-segmented), that PSC is discarded. To find the number of intersections made by a PSC, adjacent text pixels are traced along the PSC from top to bottom. If the intersection count increases to 2 then the given PSC is discarded. Wrongly segmented characters shown in Fig. 5(a) and (c) is corrected by the elimination of false PSC as shown in Fig. 5(b) and (d) respectively.

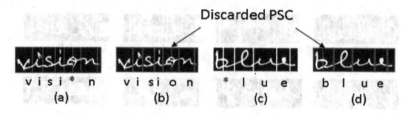

Fig. 5. (a) and (c): Wrong segmented results (b) and (d): Corrected over segmentation results.

5   Result and Discussion

In this paper self-created database consisting of 5 writers is used to test on the given algorithm along with the standard IAM dataset [5], out of which 300 non-overlapping words are chosen randomly. Segmentation results of the proposed algorithm are shown in Fig. 6. The proposed technique overcomes the problem of wrong segmentation due to the varied width of the same character as shown in Fig. 7. For the qualitative comparison of the proposed technique, the work of Amjad et al. [8] and Choudhary et al. [1] are used on the following words 'several', 'common', 'accomplish' and 'percentage' and the results are shown in Fig. 8. Method presented in [8] over segments the character like 'm' and 'n' whereas [1] miss-segments and over-segments the word like 'm', 'n', 'i' etc.

Also, it is quite difficult to compare the segmentation results with different researchers because the dataset used by everyone is different. Results achieved varies too much because some researchers assumed the absence of noise, some researchers collected the handwriting samples from a different number of writers and so on. However, for the quantitative comparison of the proposed technique, the methods presented by Salvi et al. [10] and Marti et al. [4] are considered because they have also used IAM dataset for the segmentation. The quantitative result comparison is shown in Table 1. Proposed technique fails to segment the characters if the characters are overlapping on each other, samples of wrongly segmented words with overlapping characters are shown in Fig. 9.

Table 1. Segmentation results of different methods on IAM dataset

Method	No. of words (IAM dataset)	Correctly segmented words	Wrongly segmented words	Percentage of correctly segmented words	Percentage of wrongly segmented words
Proposed method	300	255	45	85%	15%
Salvi et.al [10]	300	195	105	65%	35%
Marti et.al [4]	300	220	80	73.45%	26.55%

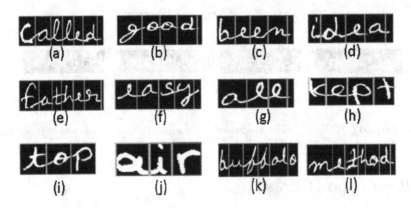

Fig. 6. Segmentation results from IAM and self-created dataset.

Fig. 7. Same word of different character width is segmented properly.

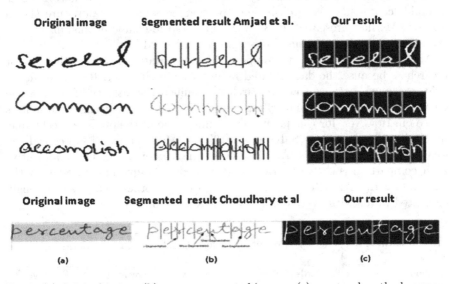

Fig. 8. (a) Original image, (b) wrong segmented images, (c) proposed method segmentation result.

Fig. 9. Wrongly segmented samples.

6   Conclusion

In this paper, an improved version of the vertical pixel count algorithm is presented. The Proposed technique was tested on IAM and self-created data set to check the efficiency of the presented algorithm. The proposed method is simple and very effective on connected text but in case of overlapping characters obtained results are not satisfactory. Further investigation will be made to handle overlapping characters by segmenting at a slope instead of vertical segmentation.

References

1. Choudhary, A., Rishi, R., Ahlawat, S.: A new character segmentation approach for off-line cursive handwritten words. Proc. Comput. Sci. **17**, 88–95 (2013)
2. Javed, M., Nagabhushan, P., Chaudhuri, B.B.: A direct approach for word and character segmentation in run-length compressed documents with an application to word spotting. In: 2015 13th International Conference on Document Analysis and Recognition (ICDAR), pp. 216–220. IEEE (2015)
3. Lee, S.W., Lee, D.J., Park, H.S.: A new methodology for gray-scale character segmentation and recognition. IEEE Trans. Pattern Anal. Mach. Intell. **18**(10), 1045–1050 (1996)
4. Marti, U.V., Bunke, H.: Text line segmentation and word recognition in a system for general writer independent handwriting recognition. In: Proceedings of Sixth International Conference on Document Analysis and Recognition, pp. 159–163. IEEE (2001)
5. Marti, U.V., Bunke, H.: The IAM-database: an English sentence database for offline handwriting recognition. Int. J. Doc. Anal. Recogn. **5**(1), 39–46 (2002)
6. Oliveira, L.S., Britto, A., Sabourin, R.: A synthetic database to assess segmentation algorithms. In: Eighth International Conference on Document Analysis and Recognition (ICDAR 2005), pp. 207–211. IEEE (2005)
7. Rehman, A., Mohamad, D., Sulong, G.: Implicit vs explicit based script segmentation and recognition: a performance comparison on benchmark database. Int. J. Open Prob. Comput. Math. **2**(3), 352–364 (2009)
8. Rehman, A., Saba, T.: Performance analysis of character segmentation approach for cursive script recognition on benchmark database. Digi. Signal Process. **21**(3), 486–490 (2011)
9. Saba, T., Rehman, A., Sulong, G.: Cursive script segmentation with neural confidence. Int. J. Innov. Comput. Inf. Contr. (IJICIC) **7**(7), 1–10 (2011)
10. Salvi, D., Zhou, J., Waggoner, J., Wang, S.: Handwritten text segmentation using average longest path algorithm. In: 2013 IEEE Workshop on Applications of Computer Vision (WACV), pp. 505–512. IEEE (2013)
11. Tulyakov, S., Govindaraju, V.: Probabilistic model for segmentation based word recognition with lexicon. In: Proceedings of Sixth International Conference on Document Analysis and Recognition. pp. 164–167. IEEE (2001)
12. Yamada, H., Nakano, Y.: Cursive handwritten word recognition using multiple segmentation determined by contour analysis. IEICE Trans. Inf. Syst. **79**(5), 464–470 (1996)

Handwriting Analysis

A Deep Learning Architecture Based Dimensionality Reduction and Online Signature Verification

Chandra Sekhar Vorugunti[(✉)] and Viswanath Pulabaigari

Indian Institute of Information Technology-SriCity, Chittoor, India
{chandrasekhar.v, viswanath.p}@iiits.in

Abstract. In this paper, we propose a novel hybrid deep learning based autoencoder-CNN-Softmax architecture aims at obtaining reduced dimension feature set from raw feature set. The reduced feature set forms an input to CNN layers to learn deep global features. These global features are used to train the SoftMax layer for online signature classification. Ability to reduce the noisy features and to discover the hidden corelated features makes the proposed architecture light weight and efficient to use in critical applications like online signature verification (OSV) and to deploy in resource constraint mobile devices. We demonstrate the superiority of our model for feature correlation learning and signature classification by conducting experiments on standard datasets MCYT, SUSIG. The experimentation confirms that the proposed model achieves better accuracy (lower error rates) with a lesser number of features compared to the current state-of-the-art models. The proposed models yield state-of-the-art performance of 0.4% EER on MCYT-100 dataset and 3.47% with SUSIG dataset.

Keywords: Dimensionality reduction · AutoEncoder · Deep learning ·
Convolution neural network · Online Signature Verification · Biometrics

1 Introduction

The advancements in Internet and mobile technologies and drastic usage of Online Signature Verification (OSV) in end to end e-transactions (online shopping, online banking etc) demands for verification models which are compact and computing efficient [1, 13, 14, 16, 17, 34]. The wide spread usage of mobile devices for OSV, intensify the problem of dimensionality reduction to discover efficient techniques to transform the high-dimensional feature set to low dimensional by learning co-related features, eliminating the redundant and noisy features with negligible loss [8, 20, 21]. The conventional dimensionality reduction techniques like principle component analysis (PCA) and multidimensional scaling (MDS) are widely used in traditional OSV [1, 2, 4, 9, 10]. These techniques are proven to excel only in case of feature set with linear data and fail to achieve accuracy in nonlinear feature sets [11, 18]. Therefore, as a solution in traditional pattern recognition space, new frame works like Isomap is proposed to overcome the limitation of PCA and MDS [33].

© Springer Nature Singapore Pte Ltd. 2019
S. Sundaram and G. Harit (Eds.): DAR 2018, CCIS 1020, pp. 109–118, 2019.
https://doi.org/10.1007/978-981-13-9361-7_10

In Deep learning space, autoencoder neural networks has been proposed to achieve higher accuracies in reducing nonlinear feature sets and finds it application in various domains [20, 21]. The advancements in MLDL [22–26, 34] techniques lead to development of autoencoder neural networks of deeper architecture and ability to process huge amount of raw feature set and reduce the dimensionality by learning an approximate identity function.

In case of traditional OSV models, Zhang et al. [1] proposed a first of its kind of an attempt for OSV based on template matching technique and achieved an Average Error Rate (AER) of 2.2% on a custom dataset. Nanni et al. [2, 3] and Porwik et al. [5] proposed OSV models based on various types of classifiers and achieved accuracies of 7.6%, 17.0% and (min: 21.56%, max: 0.2%) respectively. Van et al. [4], Fierrez et al. [6] and Sharma et al. [10] proposed OSV models based on matching techniques using viterbi path, HMM and DTW and achieved accuracies of 3.37%, 4.54% and 1.55% respectively. Cpałka et al. [12, 35], proposed OSV models based on segmenting the signature into sections called partitions and used neuro fuzzy classifier to classify the signature and models achieved an accuracies of 10.70%. and 3.24%. respectively.

Guru et al. [7, 14, 20] proposed a series of OSV models based on an interval valued symbolic representation of features of on-line signatures. In this method, Guru et al. also exploited the writer dependent threshold to classify the signature and achieved an AER of 5.7%, 1.1% and 3.8% under skilled_20 category.

Very few (only two) works have been proposed based on MLDL techniques for OSV. The first work is by Lai et al. [14], in which RNNs are trained to learn a scale invariance and rotation invariance feature called the 'length-normalized path signature', LNPS helps in classifying the signature. Lai et al. achieved an EER of 2.37% on SVC-2004 dataset. The second work is by Tolosona et al. [34], work in which a Siamese architecture based on Recurrent Neural Networks (RNNs) is proposed to learn a dissimilarity metric from the pairs of signatures. The dissimilarity metric is used to classify the signature and achieved an AER of 6.22%.

In online signature verification, no work has been done in usage of autoencoders for feature set dimensionality reduction. We are proposing a first of its kind of a deep architecture autoencoder-CNN-Softmax model in which the autoencoder reduces the feature set dimensionality by unsupervised learning of a nonlinear function to transform input to output. The reduced feature set is feed forward to CNN layers to learn deep global features. These global features are used to train the SoftMax layer for online signature classification. The model architecture is discussed in subsequent sections

2 Our Contribution

The main contributions of our work can be summarized as follows:

1. In this paper, unsupervised learning capability of an AutoEncoder neural network is used to find out and localize the correlated reduced feature set from each user/writer original features. Through dimensionality reduction, parameters (weights, bias) to be tuned are lessened and thus decreases the computational cost to train the model.

2. We present a combination of two deep neural network architectures viz., an Auto Encoder and a Convolutional Neural Network (CNN). The reduced feature set from an autoencoder is given as input to the CNN layer. CNN layer extracts the local deep features and are used for signature classification (genuine or forgery).
3. Exhaustive evaluation of the proposed model by conducting experiments on two most widely used datasets for OSV i.e. MCYT-100 and SUSIG.

The manuscript is organized as follows. In Sect. 3, we present different phases of our proposed model. In Sect. 4, details of training and testing data, experimental analysis along with the results produced by the model are discussed. A comparative analysis of the proposed model with other latest related models is reported in Sect. 5. Conclusions are drawn in Sect. 6.

3 Proposed Model Architecture

Inspired by the works from [20–27, 29, 32] in zero shot learning [20], image compressing [21], medical imaging [22, 23], human pose estimation [24], character recognition [25], feature extraction [26], anomaly detection [27], structural damage identification [29], activity recognition [32] and other critical applications like image reconstruction, missing data recovery and classification [28–31]. The fact that Auto-Encoders can reduce the feature set dimensionality effectively, and CNN can extract best local features, we combined both of them for online signature (which is a sequence of points) verification analysis. The original feature sets i.e. 100 in case of MCYT dataset and 47 in case of SUSIG forms an input to the AutoEnocder. The Autoencoder achieves an unsupervised way of learning an estimate to the identity function $h_{W,b}(x) = \hat{x} \approx x$ i.e the output values $\hat{x}$ to be equal to the input x, where W, b signifies the weights and biases respectively. Autoencoder learns the compressed or reduced representation of the input without significant information loss. The output from the AutoEncoder, a reduced feature set is feed forward to the Deep Convolutional neural network.

A neural network with more than two hidden convolutional layers can be can be considered as deep neural network. As the number of layers increases, the features extracted from lower layers are accumulated to form higher and meaningful features. We have used multilayered feed-forward Convolutional layers with 'adam' as an optimizer for back-propagation. In order to make the model to learn the features from the training data rather memorize it, we have used dropout technique with 25% and 50% dropout at each convolutional layer. This results in effective learning of features and reduces the dependency of neurons in each layers which leads to reduction of model complexity and effective learning of parameters. Apart from the dropout technique, to prevent the over-fitting we have used l1 and l2 regularizers.

Our model consists of the following components: reducing the original feature set through Autoencoders, convolutional and pooling layers, concatenation layer, fully connected layer with Sigmoid output. These fragments are discussed below:

3.1 AutoEncoder

Autoencoders are neural networks that performs dimensionality reduction on original feature set of 'm' variables to produce a set of 'n' latent variables (most important features) such that 'n' < 'm', by discovering the hidden correlated features. To perform the dimensionality reduction, the autoencoder implements an unsupervised learning of an approximate identity function $h_{W,b}(x) = \hat{x} \approx x$ with same level of reproducibility with reduced features. 'W', 'b' are parameters to be learn by the autoencoder which represents the weights and biases of the links between the hidden layers. In our model, we have used a full autoencoder i.e. the autoencoder which is trained on both genuine and forgery training samples. The reduced feature set from the autoencoder is feed forward to the convolutional neural network for further processing.

3.2 Convolution and Pooling

On receiving the reduced feature set from the autoencoder, the Convolutional Neural Network performs a one-dimensional convolution operation i.e. element-wise multiplication of each kernel/weight matrix value and the corresponding image pixel value that overlaps the weight matrix, and then take the sum of that to extract local features for each window of the given signature. Convolution operation yields a high value if the convolution feature is present in a given position, else outputs a low value. Sliding the weight matrix all over the signature feature sequence generates the advanced features, consolidating these features produce Feature Maps. In our implementation, we have used 32 filters, each of size 5 (one dimensional).

Let h: width and height of a weight matrix, c : convolution output, i : input as a matrix, w: weight matrix.

$$c_{i,j} = \sum_{p=1}^{h} \sum_{q=1}^{h} w_{p,q} * x_{i+p-1,j+q-1} \tag{1}$$

On computing the feature maps, we perform max pooling or sub sampling to make the CNN translation invariant to the input data. The sub sampling process is defined as:

$$c_{i,j} = \max\{x_{i+p-1,j+q-1}\} \text{ s.t } 1 \le p \le h \text{ and } 1 \le q \le h \tag{2}$$

3.3 Fully Connected Network with Sigmoid Output

The features generated from the last CNN layer forms input to a fully connected layer. Fully connected layer combine the local representation of the features to form a global representation of the input image/data. Sigmoid layer uses a sigmoid function (3) for binary classification. Defining mathematically, the sigmoid function will take a list of values as an input parameter, each element/value in the list will be consider as an input for the sigmoid function and will calculate the output value ranging between 0 to 1. The output values are used to determine the target class for the given test input signature. The sigmoid operation over the scores of all the classes is calculated as follows:

$$F(X)_i = \frac{1}{1 + e^{-(X_i)}} \quad i = 0, 1, 2, 3, \ldots, k \tag{3}$$

We have used 'binary_crossentropy' as the loss function that measures the discrepancy between the real signature class and the model output and 'adam' as an optimizer, with batch size of 32 and total of 400 epochs.

4 Experimentation and Results

In this segment, we present the experimental set up, results and performance analysis with the state of the art and recent literature. We have conducted the experiments on an Ubuntu machine containing Ubuntu 16.04 LTS, Intel Core i7-7700 CPU, with Titan X GPU. The proposed models are implemented in keras using python with Tensorflow [27, 32] backend.

4.1 Datasets

We have conducted experimentations on the MCYT-100 online signature dataset (DB1), Visual Subcorpus of SUSIG, dataset. The complete details of these datasets are illustrated in Table 1.

Table 1. The dataset details used in the experiments for the proposed model

DataSet →	MCYT-100	SUSIG
# of users	100	94
Total number of features	100	47
Training (genuine + training)	3600 (72%)	1880 (67%)
Testing (genuine) − FRR	700 (14%)	564 (20%)
Testing (forgery) − FAR	700 (14%)	376 (13%)
Total testing samples %	28%	33%
Total number of samples	5000	2820

Similar to [7, 11, 12], the metrics used to evaluate the efficiency of the proposed system are: (i) False Acceptance Rate (FAR), characterizes the percentage of forgeries that are accepted (FAR can be computed for each of skilled and random forgeries), (ii) False Rejection Rate (FRR), which signifies the percentage of genuine signatures that are rejected by the system, (iii) Equal Error Rate (EER), is the point at which the FRR = FAR. (iv) Average Error Rate (AER), is the average error considering FRR, FAR (random, skilled).

We have trained the system with 20 genuine signatures and with equal number of random forgery samples for each user. Genuine signatures of other writers are taken as a random forgery for a writer. Further, the training set is split into training and validation set. Sixty percent of the available training samples are used to fine tune the model. During fine tuning the model, the focus is on minimizing the Equal Error Rate (EER). Same set of hyper parameters (epochs, learning rate, batch size, number of CNN layers, dropout %, number of filters etc.) are used for testing also. We conducted experimentation for 20 number of trials and in each trial, the training and testing signatures were randomly selected.

In contrast to non-deep learning-based models [2, 3, 7, 9, 11, 12], where the models trained with 5 genuine signatures under skilled_5 category, in case of models based on deep learning, training with 5 genuine signatures doesn't lead to effective learning of parameters by the model. Hence, skilled_05 doesn't produce efficient results in AutoEncoder + CNN scenario.

We had further studied the effect of number of features considered for training the model. The EER of the proposed model of different datasets for varying number of features is shown in Tables 2 and 3. Table 2 illustrates that in case of MCYT-100 dataset, if we consider 100 features, the EER under Skilled 20 is 0.46 shown better performance compared to almost all the models presented in the literature, which considered all the 100 features. if we consider 80 features, the EER under Skilled 20 is 0.40 shown state-of-the art performance in the literature. In case of SUSIG, as depicted in Table 3, the EER resulted by considering all the 47 features is 3.92, whereas the resultant EER for 40 features is 3.61 which is best performance among the similar models except [11].

Table 2. EER (%) of the proposed autoencoder + CNN system on MCYT-100 dataset with varied number of features.

No. of training signature samples	MCYT-100 (Number of features = 100)			MCYT-100 (Number of features = 80)		
Skilled forgeries	FRR (%)	FAR (%)	EER (%)	FRR (%)	FAR (%)	EER (%)
20	0	0.92	**0.46**	0	0.8	**0.4**

Table 3. EER (%) of the proposed CNN+LSTM system on SUSIG dataset with varied number of features.

SUSIG Dataset	Number of Features = 47		Number of Features = 40	
	FRR	FAR	FRR	FAR
Average of trials	0	7.84	0	6.95
Average ERR	**3.92**		**3.47**	

Table 4. Performance comparison with the state-of-the-art methods using MCYT-100 database

Dataset-> Author	MCYT-100 (Number of features = 100) EER (%) Skilled 5	MCYT-100 (Number of features = 100) EER(%) Skilled 20
D.S. Guru et al. [12]	9.2	5.7
Manjunatha et al. [11]	19.4	1.1
D.S. Guru et al. [7]	5.8	3.8
Sharma et al. [10]	2.73	N.A.
Symbolic classifier [3]	5.8	3.8
Linear programing description (LPD) [3]	9.4	5.6
Nearest neighbor description (NND) [3]	12.2	6.3
Principal component analysis description (PCAD) [3]	7.9	4.2
Support vector description (SVD) [3]	8.9	5.4
Parzen window classifier (PWC) [3]	9.7	5.2
Gaussian model description [3]	7.7	4.4
Random ensemble of base (RS) [2]	9.0	–
Random subspace ensemble with resampling of base (RSB) [2]	9.0	9.0
Base classifier (BASE) [3]	17.0	–
Regularized Parzen window classifier RPWC [2]	9.7	–
Ensemble of Parzen window classifier [3]	8.4	2.9
Mixture of Gaussian description_3(MOGD_3) [3]	8.9	7.3
Cpałka et al. [9]	4.88	–
Zalasińskia et al. [16]	3.14	–
Cpałka et al. [15]	5.20	–
Proposed – Considering 100 features.	N.A.	**(FRR = 0 + FAR = 0.92)/2 = 0.46**
Proposed – Considering 80 features.	N.A.	**(FRR = 0 + FAR = 0.8)/2 = 0.4**

Table 5. Performance comparison with the state-of-the-art methods using SUSIG database

Dataset-> Author	SUSIG (Number of features = 47) EER (%) Skilled 10
Yuen et al. [35]	8.72
Yanikoglu et al. [19]	6.20
Napa Sae-Bae et al. [8]	6.08
Napa Sae-Bae et al. (including histogram in feature set) [8]	4.37
Pirlo et al. [36]	3.88
Manjunatha et al. [11]	1.92
Proposed (40 features)	**(FRR = 0 + FAR = 6.95)/2 = 3.47**

5   Comparative Study

To demonstrate the effectiveness of the proposed model, we have considered the OSV models which are validated on similar datasets SUSIG and MCYT data corpus (DB1). Further, the models considered for evaluation have utilized all the features while training the model. On the contrary, our model works in lower dimension. From Table 4, it is clear that the proposed model have achieved state of the art EER under both the categories of 100 and 80 features. Therefore, our model saved the computational complexity of 20 (features) *50 (signatures) * 100(users) = 10000 features, which predominantly reduces the computational and storage complexity of the model. The reason for not performing the experimentation under Skilled-05 category is that the 5 signature per user is predominantly lesser for a deep learning-based model to learn the weights effectively. Table 5 confirms that in case of SUISG, the proposed model which is trained on 40 features, out performs all the models which are trained with 47 features except [11].

6   Conclusion

In this manuscript we proposed a first, complete and successful framework of its kind by combining two deep learning architectures AutoEncoder and CNN. The correlated features extracted by the AutoEncoder forms an input to the CNN. The proposed model is thoroughly tested on multiple datasets and proved its efficiency with reduced error rates. In case of MCYT-Skilled 20 category, the proposed model achieved the state-of-the art EER value which reduced feature set, indicating the AutoEncoder + CNN technique has potential to develop efficient and light weight models for OSV. Future work could explore the integration LSTM to the existing model to learn temporal dependency among the features.

References

1. Zhang, K., Nyssen, E., Sahli, H.: Multi-stage online signature verification system. Pattern Anal. Appl. **5**, 288–295 (2001)
2. Nanni, L., Lumini, A.: Advanced methods for two-class problem formulation for online signature verification. Neurocomputing. **69**, 854–857 (2006)
3. Nanni, L.: Experimental comparison of one-class classifiers for on-line signature verification. Neuro. Comput. **69**, 869–873 (2006)
4. Van, B.L., Garcia-Salicetti, S., Dorizzi, B.: On using the viterbi path along with HMM likelihood information for online signature verification. IEEE Trans. Syst. Man Cybern. Part B **37**(5), 1237–1247 (2007)
5. Porwik, P., Doroz, R., Orczyk, T.: Signatures verification based on PNN classifier optimised by PSO algorithm. Pattern Recogn. **60**, 998–1014 (2016)
6. Fierrez, J., Ortega-Garcia, J., Ramos, D., Gonzalez-Rodriguez, J.: HMM-based on-line signature verification: feature extraction and signature modeling. Pattern Recogn. Lett. **28** (16), 2325–2334 (2007)
7. Guru, D.S., Prakash, H.N.: Online signature verification and recognition: an approach based on symbolic representation. IEEE Trans. Pattern Anal. Mach. Intell. **31**, 1059–1073 (2009)
8. Napa, S., Nasir, M.: Online signature verification on mobile devices. IEEE Trans. Inf. Forensics Secur. **9**, 933–947 (2014)
9. Cpałka, K., Zalasinski, M., Rutkowski, L.: A new algorithm for identity verification based on the analysis of a handwritten dynamic signature. Appl. Soft Comput. **43**, 47–56 (2016)
10. Sharma, A., Sundaram, S.: An enhanced contextual DTW based system for online signature verification using vector quantization. Pattern Recogn. Lett. **84**, 22–28 (2016)
11. Manjunatha, K.S., Manjunath, S., Guru, D.S., Somashekara, M.T.: Online signature verification based on writer dependent features and classifiers. Pattern Recogn. Lett. **80**, 129–136 (2016)
12. Guru, D.S., Manjunatha, K.S., Manjunath, S., Somashekara, M.T.: Interval valued symbolic representation of writer dependent features for online signature verification. Elsevier J. Expert Syst. Appl. **80**, 232–243 (2017)
13. Alpar, O., Krejcar, O.: Online signature verification by spectrogram analysis. J. Appl. Intell **48**, 1189–1199 (2018)
14. Lai, S., Jin, L., Yang, W.: Online signature verification using recurrent neural network and length-normalized path signature descriptor. In: 14th IAPR International Conference on Document Analysis and Recognition (ICDAR), Kyoto, Japan (2017)
15. Cpałka, K., Zalasinski, M.: On-line signature verification using vertical signature partitioning. Expert Syst. Appl. **41**, 4170–4180 (2014)
16. Zalasińskia, M., Cpałkaa, K.: A new method for signature verification based on selection of the most important partitions of the dynamic signature. J. Neurocomput. **289**, 13–22 (2018)
17. Xia, X., Song, X., Luan, F., Zheng, J., Chen, Z., Ma, X.: Discriminative feature selection for on-line signature verification. Pattern Recogn. **74**, 422–433 (2018)
18. Wang, J., He, H., Danil, V., Prokhorov, A.: Folded neural network autoencoder for dimensionality reduction. In: International Neural Network Society Winter Conference INNS-WC 2012 (2012)
19. Yanikoglu, B., Kholmatov, A.: Online signature verification using Fourier descriptors. EURASIP J. Adv. Signal Process. **1**, 260516 (2009)
20. Mishra, A., Reddy, S., Mittal, A., Hema Murthy, A.: A generative model for zero shot learning using conditional variational autoencoders. In: International Conference on Pattern Recognition CVPR (2018)

21. David, A., Chih-Peng, C., Wen-Hsiao, P., Hsueh-Ming, H.: An auto encoder-based learned image compressor: description of challenge proposal by NCTU. In: CVPR, Salt lake, USA (2018)
22. Yildirim, O., San Tan, R., Rajendra Acharya, U.: An efficient compression of ECG signals using deep convolutional autoencoders. Elsevier J. Cogn. Syst. Res. **52**, 198–211 (2018)
23. Adem, K., Kiliçarslan, S., Cömert, O.: Classification and diagnosis of cervical cancer with softmax classification with stacked autoencoder. Elsevier J. Expert Syst. Appl. **115**, 557–564 (2019)
24. Trumble, M., Gilbert, A., Hilton, A., Collomosse, J.: Deep Autoencoder for Combined Human Pose Estimation and Body Model Upscaling. In: Ferrari, V., Hebert, M., Sminchisescu, C., Weiss, Y. (eds.) ECCV 2018. LNCS, vol. 11214, pp. 800–816. Springer, Cham (2018). https://doi.org/10.1007/978-3-030-01249-6_48
25. Anupriya, G., Angshul, M.: Discriminative autoencoder for feature extraction: application to character recognition. Neural Process. Lett. **49**, 1–13 (2018)
26. Chen, J., Cheng Wua, Z., Zhang, J.: Driver identification based on hidden feature extraction by using adaptive non negativity-constrained auto encoder. Appl. Soft Comput. J. **74**, 1–9 (2019)
27. Narasimhan, M.G., Kamath, S.: Dynamic video anomaly detection and localization using sparse denoising auto encoders. Multimedia Tools Appl. **77**, 13173–13195 (2018)
28. Nath, A., Karthikeyan, S.: Enhanced prediction of recombination hotspots using input features extracted by class specific auto encoders. J. Theor. Biol. **444**, 73–82 (2018)
29. Pathirage, C.S., Li, J., Li, L., Hao, H., Liu, W., Ni, P.: Structural damage identification based on auto encoder neural networks and deep learning. Eng. Struct. **172**, 13–28 (2018)
30. Feng, S., Duarte, M.: Graph auto encoder-based unsupervised feature selection with broad and local data structure preservation. Elsevier J. Neuro. Comput. **000**, 1–14 (2018)
31. Deng, Y., Sander, A., Faulstich, L., Denecke, K.: Towards automatic encoding of medical procedures using convolutional neural networks and auto encoders. Elsevier J. Artif. Intell. Med. **93**, 29–42 (2019)
32. Ibrahim, M.S., Mori, G.: Hierarchical relational networks for group activity recognition and retrieval. In: 5th European Conference on Computer Vision (ECCV), 8–14 September 2018
33. Yan, Z., Zhao, Z., Jie, Q., Li, Z., Bing, L., Fanzhang, L.: Semi-supervised local multi-manifold isomap by linear embedding for feature extraction. Pattern Recogn. **76**, 662–678 (2018)
34. Tolosana, R., Vera-Rodriguez, R., Fierrez, J., Ortega-Garcia, J.: Exploring recurrent neural networks for on-line handwritten signature biometrics. IEEE Access **6**, 5128–5138 (2018)
35. Yuen, C.T., Lim, W.L., Tan, C.S., Goi, B.M., Wang, X., Ho, J.H., Probabilistic model for dynamic signature verification system, J. Appl. Sci. Eng. Technol. **3**, 1318–1322 (2011)
36. Pirlo, G., Cuccovillo, V., Cabrera, M.D., Impedovo, D., Mignone, P.: Multidomain verification of dynamic signatures using local stability analysis. IEEE Trans. Hum. Mach. Syst. **45**, 805–810 (2015)

Word-Wise Handwriting Based Gender Identification Using Multi-Gabor Response Fusion

Maryam Asadzadeh Kaljahi[1], P. V. Vidya Varshini[2],
Palaiahnakote Shivakumara[1(⊠)], Umapada Pal[3], Tong Lu[4],
and D. S. Guru[5]

[1] Faculty of Computer Science and Information Technology,
University of Malaya, Kuala Lumpur, Malaysia
{asadzadeh,shiva}@um.edu.my
[2] Vellore Institute of Technology, Vellore, Tamil Nadu, India
vidyavarshini.pv2015@vit.ac.in
[3] Computer Vision and Pattern Recognition Unit,
Indian Statistical Institute, Kolkata, India
umapada@isical.ac.in
[4] National Key Lab for Novel Software Technology,
Nanjing University, Nanjing, China
lutong@nju.edu.cn
[5] Department of Studies in Computer Science, Manasagangotri,
University of Mysuru, Mysore, India
dsg@compsci.uni-mysore.ac.in

Abstract. Handwriting based gender identification at the word level is challenging due to free style writing, use of different scripts, and inadequate information. This paper presents a new method based on Multi-Gabor Response (MGR) fusion for gender identification at the word level. It first explores weighted-gradient features for word segmentation from text line images. For each word, the proposed method obtains eight Gabor response images. Then it performs sliding window operation over MGR images to smooth the values. For each smoothed MGR images, we perform fusion operation that chooses the Gabor response value which contributes to the highest peak in the histogram. This process results in a feature matrix, which is fed to CNN for gender identification. Experimental results on our dataset (multi scripts) apart from English, and benchmark databases, namely, IAM, KHATT, and QUWI, which contain handwritten English and Arabic text, show that the proposed method outperforms the existing methods.

Keywords: Zero crossing points · Word segmentation · Gabor responses ·
Multi-Gabor response fusion · Convolutional neural networks ·
Gender identification

© Springer Nature Singapore Pte Ltd. 2019
S. Sundaram and G. Harit (Eds.): DAR 2018, CCIS 1020, pp. 119–132, 2019.
https://doi.org/10.1007/978-981-13-9361-7_11

1 Introduction

As crime rate increases exponentially at city levels, the complexity of identifying fraud or fake documents related crimes also increases in the field of document image analysis. One such challenge is handwriting based gender identification because of free style writing, different orientations variety of scripts etc. On the other hand, gender identification is useful in several real time applications, namely, document authorization, establishing the authenticity of historical handwriting samples, and identifying a disorder or abnormal [1, 2]. There are different ways for gender identification in literature. Graphology based methods [2] explore geometrical characteristics of individual characters. Non-biometric based methods use text, speech, socio political, environmental context, dressing style, hairstyle, etc., for gender identification. Soft biometric based methods use height, weight, eye color, silhouette, age, gender, race, moles, tattoos, birthmarks, scars, etc. Biometric based methods explore face, iris, ear, fingerprint, voice, gait, gesture, lip motion handwriting writing style, etc. It is noted that these methods suffer from their inherent limitations to achieve good results. For instance, graphology based methods are limited to specific applications because hypothesis and rules are derived based on pseudo-scientific [3]. Similarly, non-biometric, soft biometric and biometric based methods are not robust or reliable when images are affected by external adverse factors caused by open environments.

The above observations motivated us to introduce handwriting for gender identification. This is because in contrast to face recognition, person behavior identification and speech processing, capturing and processing handwriting images do not require high computations. Furthermore, handwriting based gender identification is more reliable compared to the above methods. Although most of the existing methods are proposed for gender identification using handwriting analysis [4], these methods require a few text lines or the whole page, at least the full text line containing a few words for achieving good results. This process not only requires more computations but also annoying for a person to write one page or many lines during creating a dataset. In addition, free and unconstrained writing makes the problem more challenging. Hence, in this work, we propose a new method for handwriting based gender identification at word level based on the fact that female writing is legible and visible compared to male writing. It is evident from the samples given in Fig. 1, where one can see differences between female and male writing irrespective of scripts, background, paper, ink, etc.

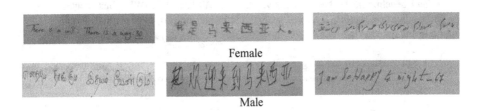

Female

Male

Fig. 1. Samples of female and male handwriting in different scripts, orientations and backgrounds.

2   Related Work

The proposed method includes word segmentation from text lines and gender identification at the word level. Therefore, we present a review of word segmentation and gender identification in this section.

Wshah et al. [5] proposed segmentation of Arabic handwriting based on both contour and skeleton segmentation. The method divides each whole component into smaller units and then constructs lexicons for segmenting words from Arabic text lines. Since the performance of the method depends on skeleton and contour, it is sensitive to disconnections. Louloudis et al. [6] proposed text line and word segmentation of handwritten documents. The method first obtains a binary image for the input text line. Then it studies the distance between character components in the text line. However, the method is ineffective for other scripts such as Arabic and Indian scripts, where we cannot expect the uniform spacing between characters and words. Osman [7] proposed a segmentation algorithm for Arabic handwritten texts based on contour analysis. The method traces contours of components to study the direction. However, the conditions and rules proposed work well for Arabic but not for other scripts. Banumathi and Chandra [8] proposed line and word segmentation of Kannada handwritten text documents using projection profiles. This idea works well when the space between words is greater than that between characters. This constraint may not be true for handwriting all the time. Recently, Khare et al. [9] proposed weighted gradient features for hand-written line segmentation. The method is developed to overcome the issue of touching between lines. Though the method is robust to noise and touching, the scope is limited to text line segmentation but not word segmentation.

In light of the above discussions, it observed that most of the methods use the output of binarization methods, which work based on thresholding. Similarly, the majority of the methods focused text lines of a particular script but not multiple scripts. In addition, the methods hardly addressed the issue of word segmentation especially, for Arabic and Indian scripts. Therefore, there is a scope for developing a method that works well for word segmentation irrespective of scripts and background complexities. Hence, this paper, inspired by the method [9] where the weighed gradient is explored for text line segmentation, we explore the same for word segmentation in a new way.

In the same way of word segmentation methods, there are methods for gender identification using handwriting analysis. Bouadjenek et al. [10] proposed age, gender and handedness prediction from handwriting using gradient features. The method proposes to combine HOG, LBP and pixel density based features for classification. It is good for high contrast images. Maji et al. [11] proposed effect of Euler number as a feature in their gender recognition system from offline handwritten signature using neural networks. The performance of the method depends on the output of binarization. Mirza et al. [12] proposed gender classification from offline handwriting images using textural features. The method uses Gabor filters for extracting texture features of handwriting images. It is sensitive to different orientations of text lines. Tan et al. [13] proposed a multi-feature selection of handwriting for gender identification using mutual information. The method extracts different features such as geometrical and transformed ones for input images. However, extracted features are not robust to disconnections and noises. Akbari et al. [14] proposed wavelet-based gender detection on offline handwritten documents using probabilistic finite state automata. The method proposes wavelet decomposition for extracting texture features for input images. However, the method is limited to a particular script.

Recently, Navya et al. [3] proposed multi-gradient directional features for gender identification. The method checks converging criteria for successive text lines. If the process converges then the input document is classified as female else male. However, since the gradient mask values are fixed, the performance of the method is not effective. Therefore, to overcome this issue, the same authors proposed adaptive multi-gradient kernels for handwriting based gender identification [15]. The method uses local information to calculate automatic mask values. It follows the same as the previous method for gender classification. However, the above methods require at least three successive text lines for gender identification. As a result, the method cannot be used at text line level or word level. Moetesum et al. [16] proposed data driven feature extraction for gender classification using multi-script handwritten texts. The method explores convolutional neural network for feature extraction, and then uses linear discriminate analysis for classification. It considers Arabic and English scripts for gender identification and reports classification rates at the word level. However, the results reported at the word level are poor. In addition, the scope of the method is limited to only two scripts.

In summary, most of these methods use local foreground information such as character shape, geometrical features or appearances of characters, and texture of character appearances in addition to classifiers for gender identification. As a result, the features are not robust to multiple scripts at the word level. Besides, the existing methods are tested on a maximum two scripts but not more scripts, which only include English and Arabic. Therefore, we can assert that there is a huge gap between the existing methods and gender identification at the word level, where one can expect multiple scripts due to multi-lingual countries like India and Malaysia.

Hence, in this paper, we propose a new method by exploring Multiple Gabor Responses (MGR) and fusion of MGR images. It is true that the difference between female and male writing can be seen predominantly in the direction of contours. To extract such observation, we explore Gabor responses of different orientations [17]. For segmenting words from multiscript text lines, inspired by the method [9] where weighed gradient features are used for line segmentation, we explore the same in a different way for word segmentation.

3   Proposed Method

Since the aim of the proposed work is to identify gender at the word level irrespective of scripts, backgrounds and orientations, we propose two steps, namely, the method for word segmentation from text lines, and gender identification using segmented words.

It is true that word segmentation from English text line is easier than Arabic, Farsi and Indian scripts because one can expect regular spacing for English, while for other scripts, it does not (see Fig. 1). In the case of Arabic and Farsi, due to the presences of diacritics and special calligraphic symbols, it is hard to find the space and exact words in text lines [16]. To alleviate this problem, we explore weighted gradient information, which helps us to separate extreme pixels at top and bottom from the middle pixels of a text line, and hence facilitates word segmentation properly. This is because the step works based on the fact that the number of zero crossing points at middle rows is larger than those at top and bottom of the text line.

In general, we believe that female handwritings have consistency and unique, while for male writing, one cannot predict writing styles [16]. To extract such observation, we propose Multi-Gabor Responses (MGR) because of the fact that direction information is more sensitive to the style of writing than the magnitude of pixel values. In this work, we consider 8 directions of Gabor responses because we believe that the above 8 directions provide prominent information for separating female and male writing. Then, we propose fusion operation to combine the 8 MGR images as one fused image, which results in a feature matrix. Due to the strong discriminating ability of Convolutional Neural Networks (CNN) [18], finally, we propose to use the same for gender identification in this work.

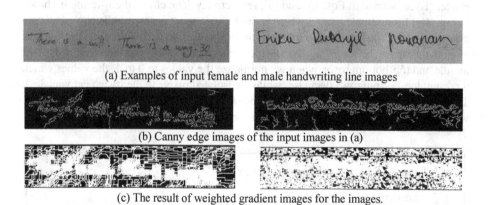

(a) Examples of input female and male handwriting line images

(b) Canny edge images of the input images in (a)

(c) The result of weighted gradient images for the images.

Fig. 2. Enhancing the values of middle pixels while suppressing top and bottom pixels of text lines of female and male.

3.1   Word Segmentation

For the female and male handwritten text line images shown in Fig. 2(a), the proposed method obtains Canny edge images as shown in Fig. 2(b). With the Canny edge images, the proposed method counts the number of zero crossing points (0 to 1 and 1 to 0) for every row, which is considered as weight. The weights of the respective rows are multiplied with the gradient values of pixels of the rows as defined in Eq. (1). This gives weighted gradient images as defined in Eq. (2). The effect of weighted gradient values can be seen in Fig. 2(c), where we can see pixels of middle rows are enhanced compared to those of bottom and top rows. The same conclusion can be drawn from the histograms drawn for weighted gradient values shown in Fig. 3, where we can see the high peak for the values of middle rows and low peaks for the top-bottom rows.

$$W_i = \sum_{j=1}^{y} C_{i,j} \tag{1}$$

where W_i is the weight of ith row, where y is the number of columns in the canny image C and $C_{i,j} = \{0, 1\}$

$$WG_{i,j} = W_i \times G_{i,j} \tag{2}$$

where $WG_{i,j}$ is the weighted gradient of each pixel (i,j) in the weighted gradient image, and $G_{i,j}$ is gradient magnitude of each pixel.

In case of handwriting, ascenders and descenders in English, and diacritics or calligraphic symbols in Arabic or Farsi pose problems for segmenting words from text lines, which are considered as extreme pixels. To reduce the impact of such pixels, we propose to deploy k-means clustering with k = 2 on normalized weighted gradient values, which classifies high values into a Max cluster (A) and low values into a Min cluster (B) as defined in Eqs. (3) and (4), respectively. The effect of clustering is shown in Fig. 4(a) for a female image, where it can be seen most of the middle row pixels are classified into a Max cluster and top-bottom row pixels into a Min cluster. This helps us to find the space between words. Besides, due to the wide gap between values of middle and top-bottom rows, when we normalize the values to 0 to 1, the values which represent top-bottom rows decrease, while the isolated pixels in the image get vanished. Therefore, noisy pixels present in Canny edge images shown in Fig. 2(b) are removed, which can be seen in Fig. 4(a). This is the advantage of weighted gradient values.

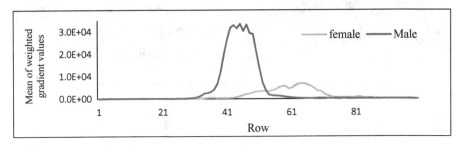

Fig. 3. Middle pixels are enhanced compared to top and bottom pixels of texts of female and male.

However, sometimes, the clustering may disconnect components due to the separation of middle and bottom-top row pixels and multi-orientation of text lines. Therefore, we perform a morphological operation to fill the single pixel gap as shown in Fig. 4(b). To merge sub-components as a word component, we perform grouping by merging components that have overlapping bounding boxes as shown in Fig. 4(c). To restore the missing information if any due to the above process, the proposed method compares the area of the bounding boxes (X) in Max and Min clusters, and chooses the patch that gives a larger size as a word patch as defined in Eq. (5). It is illustrated in

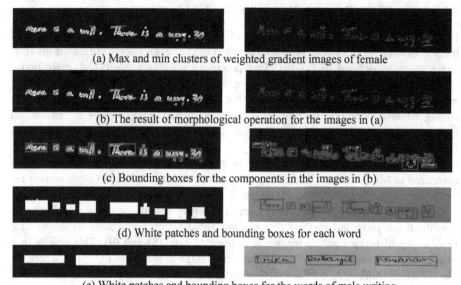

(a) Max and min clusters of weighted gradient images of female

(b) The result of morphological operation for the images in (a)

(c) Bounding boxes for the components in the images in (b)

(d) White patches and bounding boxes for each word

(e) White patches and bounding boxes for the words of male writing

Fig. 4. Word segmentation for the female and male handwriting.

Fig. 4(d), where it is noted that each white patch represents a word. The final word separation results are shown with the bounding boxes in Fig. 4(d). In the same way, the proposed method segments words for male writing as the shown samples in Fig. 4(e), where one can see all the words are separated properly.

$$A_{i,j} = \begin{cases} WG_{i,j} & \text{if k means}(WG_{i,j}) = \text{cluster}_{max} \\ 0 & \text{otherwise} \end{cases} \tag{3}$$

$$B_{i,j} = \begin{cases} WG_{i,j} & \text{if k means}(WG_{i,j}) = \text{cluster}_{min} \\ 0 & \text{otherwise} \end{cases} \tag{4}$$

where $WG_{i,j}$ denote weighted gradient matrix.

$$M_{i,j} = \begin{cases} 1 & \text{if intersection}\left(X_{Min}^{i} \ and \ X_{Max}^{j}\right) = \text{True} \\ 0 & \text{otherwise} \end{cases} \tag{5}$$

Note that for English texts, usually, the patches in the Max cluster has a larger size than those in the Min cluster, while for Arabic and Farsi, it is vice versa sometimes. In this way, the patches of Max and Min clusters are useful in handling the issue of the multi-script scenarios.

3.2   Multi-Gabor Response Fusion for Gender Identification

For each input segmented word image of female and male writing, the proposed method obtains 8 Gabor responses as discussed in [17] at an interval of 25° from 180° angle space as defined in Eq. (6). This process results in 8 Multi-Gabor Response (MGR) images as shown in Fig. 5, where we can see the prominent information is reflected in 8 directions. To normalize the values, the proposed method performs sliding window operation for respective 8 MGR images, and chooses the maximum element from each sliding window. This results in MGR smoothed images as defined in Eq. (7), which are illustrated in Fig. 5. It is observed from MGR images and MGR smoothed images in Fig. 5 that the values in MGR smoothed images are sharpened compared to MGR images. In order to integrate the strength of each Gabor responses, the proposed method performs histogram operation for each sliding window of size 3 × 3 across 8 MGR smoothed images. For every sliding window of histogram operation, the proposed method chooses the value which contributes to the highest peak in the histogram as the feature as defined in Eqs. (8) and (9). This results in a fused image of the same dimension of the input image as shown in Fig. 5(c), where we can see a clear difference between female and male writings, which is the feature matrix for gender identification.

$$R(x, y; w, \alpha) = \exp\left\{\frac{-1}{2}\left[\frac{x'}{\beta_x^2} + \frac{y'}{\beta_y^2}\right]\right\}\cos(2\pi wx') \tag{6}$$

$$x' = x\sin\varepsilon + y\cos\varepsilon$$
$$y' = x\cos\varepsilon - y\sin\varepsilon$$

where, w is the frequency of wave propagating in the direction of ε from x-axis, while β_x and β_y define Gaussian envelope along with the respective axes.

$$E_{i,j}^g = \max\left(R_{r,r'}^g\right) \quad \text{where } r \in \{i-1, i, i+1\} \text{ and } r' \in \{j-1, j, j+1\} \tag{7}$$

where $E_{i,j}^g$ is the enhanced value of pixel (i,j) of the gth R image, and is the maximum value in a 3 by 3 window with the center as (i,j).

$$\eta_{i,j} = max^{frequency}\left[Histogram\left(R_{r,r'}^\mu\right)\right] \quad where \ \mu \in \{1, 2, \ldots, 8\} \tag{8}$$

$$F_{i,j} = \mathcal{R}(\eta_{i,j}) \tag{9}$$

where $\eta_{i,j}$ is the maximum frequency belongs to pixel (i, j) in a histogram of 72 values from all the 3 × 3 windows of R images in the same location. $\mathcal{R}(\eta_{i,j})$ determines the pixel value that leads to $\eta_{i,j}$ and would be a feature in the final feature image called F.

It is true that CNN has the ability to learn parameters with a few numbers of samples [18]. Therefore, the obtained feature matrix is passed to fully connected

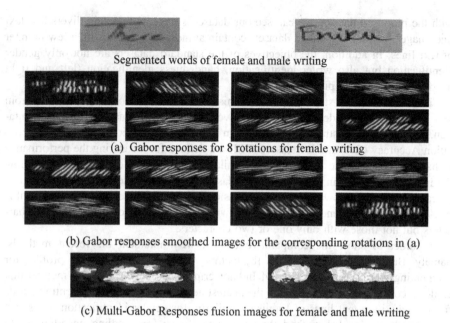

Segmented words of female and male writing

(a) Gabor responses for 8 rotations for female writing

(b) Gabor responses smoothed images for the corresponding rotations in (a)

(c) Multi-Gabor Responses fusion images for female and male writing

Fig. 5. Multi-Gabor responses for feature extraction of female and male writing.

Convolutional Neural Network (CNN) for gender classification. For choosing samples for training and testing, we follow standard 10-fold cross validation. In this work, we consider the following parameters for training and testing: 100 hidden layers, 100 neurons, 1000 iterations, Penalty weights 1.0E-8, and hidden layer dropout rate as 0.5. All these parameters are determined experimentally according to pre-defined labeled data.

4 Experimental Results

Since there is no standard dataset for multi-script data that includes English, Arabic, Farsi, Chinese and Indian script, we create our own dataset for experimentation in this work. Our dataset includes free writing styles, which has different orientations, backgrounds, papers, inks and text lines written by different aged people from 10–70 years old. In total, the dataset contains 2278 female writing and 1026 male writing, which gives 3304 text line images. To show the effectiveness of the proposed method, we also test it on benchmark databases, namely, IAM which contains English text lines, KHATT which contains Arabic text lines, and QUWI which contains both English and Arabic [4]. The IAM dataset provides 100 testing samples per class, KHATT dataset provides 45 testing samples per class, while QUWI dataset provides 250 samples per class. Overall, 3304 from our database, 200 from IAM database, 90 from KHATT database and 500 from QUWI database, which gives 4094 text line images for evaluating the proposed and existing methods. When we compare the standard datasets with the proposed dataset, we can see our dataset is huge and contain diversified text line images, while the standard datasets contain at most two scripts with a few number of text lines. In addition, the objectives of the standard datasets are not only gender identification but also writer identification, handedness identification (left and right hand writing) and age prediction [4].

There are two key steps proposed in this work, namely, word segmentation from text lines and gender identification at the word level. For evaluating word segmentation, we follow the instructions provided in [9], where Detection Rate (DR), Recognition Accuracy (RA) and F-Measure (FM) are defined for measuring the performance of handwriting text line segmentation. Similarly, for gender identification, we follow the instructions given in [16], where the classification rate is defined for gender classification. In addition, we report the confusion matrix of gender classification in this work. Note that for gender identification, we consider words containing a few characters but not those with only one or two characters.

In order to show the comparative results, we implement the recent methods, namely, Banumathi and Chandra's [8] method that explores projection profiles for segmenting words from text lines of Indian script. Louloudis et al.'s [6] method that explores connected components and the nearest neighbor criteria for segmenting words from handwritten text lines of English. Similarly, for gender identification, we select Bouadjenek et al.'s [4] method that introduces fuzzy for handling uncertainties to improve results of classification, and Bouadjenek et al.'s [10] method that explores gradient, LBP and HOG descriptors for feature extraction and an SVM classifier for classification. The reason to consider the above methods for comparative study is as follows: the method in [8] focuses on segmenting words from text lines of Indian script as the proposed method, the method in [6] focuses on English text for word segmentation, the method in [4] aims at handling uncertainties caused by multiple scripts, while the method in [10] explores well-known descriptors for gender identification at text line level.

4.1 Experiments on Word Segmentation

Sample qualitative results of the proposed method for word segmentation on different datasets are shown in Fig. 6, where it is noted that the proposed method works well irrespective of scripts, background and orientations. Quantitative results on line segmentation of the proposed and existing methods for our and the existing standard datasets are reported in Table 1, where it is observed that the proposed method is the best at DR, RA and FM for all the datasets compared to the existing methods. However, since the existing methods target particular scripts, they do not perform well. It is noted from Table 1 that the method including the proposed method reports the lowest for KHATT. This is because KHATT provides only Arabic text lines, which is not so easy for word segmenting compared to English and other scripts. At the same time, for IAM dataset which contains English, the methods score the highest results.

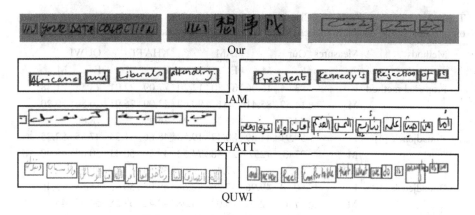

Fig. 6. Qualitative results of the proposed word segmentation on our and standard datasets

Table 1. Performance of the proposed and existing methods for line segmentation on different datasets.

Methods	Proposed Method			Banumathi [8]			Louloudis [6]		
DataSet	DR	RA	FM	DR	RA	FM	DR	RA	FM
Our dataset	**65.00**	**79.44**	**71.50**	14.55	40.0	21.33	28.18	62.0	38.75
IAM	**93.51**	**81.40**	**87.03**	55.99	77.65	65.06	70.36	46.19	55.77
KHATT	**45.0**	**52.94**	**48.65**	10.37	56.00	17.50	30.36	47.71	37.11
QUWI	**52.32**	**74.93**	**61.61**	14.66	47.16	22.35	44.58	37.65	40.82

4.2   Experiments on Gender Identification

Quantitative results of the proposed and existing methods for gender identification on our and the existing standard datasets are reported in Table 2, where we can see the proposed method is the best compared to the existing methods in terms of classification rate for all the datasets. The reason for the poor results of the existing methods is that the methods [4, 10] are developed for text lines but not words. When we compare the results of the existing methods, the method [4] scores better results than [10] because the former has the ability to handle uncertainties of classification, while the latter does not have. However, since the proposed method extracts directional features and CNN for classification, it is better than all the existing methods. The methods including the proposed method score the best for IAM and the worst for KHATT. This is due to KHATT provides only Arabic while another dataset provides mixed of female and male writings.

Qualitative results of the proposed method for gender classification are shown in Fig. 7(a) and (b) where we can see the method classifies successfully and unsuccessfully for some images, which share the same properties. Due to the presence of diacritics and special calligraphic symbols as shown in Fig. 8 where we can see it is hard to find the word from naked eyes. Therefore, it is required recognition of characters and meaning for successful segmentation. This is beyond the scope of the work.

Table 2. Confusion matrix and Classification Rate (CR) of the proposed and existing methods on our dataset and standard datasets. Here F denotes Female and M denoted Male writings.

Methods	Measures	Our		IAM		KHATT		QUWI	
		F	M	F	M	F	M	F	M
Proposed method	F	83.94	16.06	87.80	12.20	77.09	22.91	78.52	21.48
	M	14.59	85.41	9.31	90.69	23.09	76.91	20.80	79.20
	CR	**84.71**		**89.24**		**76.99**		**78.86**	
Bouadjenek [4]	F	58.91	41.09	80.42	19.58	48.66	51.34	47.65	52.35
	M	2743	7257	25.48	74.52	49.59	50.41	50.60	49.40
	CR	65.73		77.47		49.53		48.52	
Bouadjenek [10]	F	50.04	49.96	57.36	42.64	49.05	50.95	56.55	43.45
	M	47.43	52.57	45.02	54.98	42.42	57.58	54.55	45.45
	CR	51.30		56.17		53.32		51	

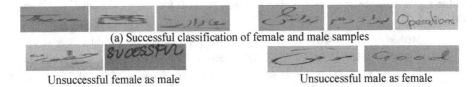

(a) Successful classification of female and male samples

Unsuccessful female as male   Unsuccessful male as female

Fig. 7. Qualitative results of proposed method for gender identification

Fig. 8. Limitation of the proposed segmentation step especially for Arabic, Farsi scripts.

5   Conclusion and Future Work

In this paper, we present a new method for handwriting based gender identification at the word level. The proposed method explores weighted gradients for word segmentation from handwritten text lines, which involves the number of zero crossing points of every row. Multi-Gabor responses are proposed for feature extraction from segmented word images. We propose fusion operation for obtaining the fused image from multi-Gabor smoothed images. This results in a feature matrix. Furthermore, the convolutional neural network is used for gender identification at the word level. Experimental results on our own dataset and three standard datasets with comparative studies for word segmentation and gender identification show that the proposed method is effective and useful. However, there are still limitations of word segmentation especially for Arabic and Farsi scripts as discussed in the Experimental Section. Similarly, when words are oriented arbitrarily, the performance of the proposed on gender identification degrades. These are the future issues to extend the proposed work.

Acknowledgement. This work was supported by the Natural Science Foundation of China under Grant 61672273 and Grant 61832008, and the Science Foundation for Distinguished Young Scholars of Jiangsu under Grant BK20160021.

References

1. Kalsi, K.S., Rai, P.: A classification of emotion and gender using approximation image Gabor local binary pattern. In: 7th International Conference on Cloud Computing, Data Science & Engineering, pp 623–628. IEEE (2017)
2. Topaloglu, M., Ekmekci, S.: Gender detection and identifying one's handwriting with handwriting analysis. Expert Syst. Appl. **79**, 236–243 (2017)
3. Navya, B., et al.: Multi-gradient directional features for gender identification. In: 24th International Conference on Pattern Recognition (ICPR), pp. 3657–3662. IEEE (2018)
4. Bouadjenek, N., Nemmour, H., Chibani, Y.: Robust soft-biometrics prediction from off-line handwriting analysis. Appl. Soft Comput. **46**, 980–990 (2016)
5. Wshah, S., Shi, Z., Govindaraju, V.: Segmentation of Arabic handwriting based on both contour and skeleton segmentation. In: 10th International Conference on Document Analysis and Recognition ICDAR 2009, pp. 793–797. IEEE (2009)
6. Louloudis, G., Gatos, B., Pratikakis, I., Halatsis, C.: Text line and word segmentation of handwritten documents. Pattern Recogn. **42**(12), 3169–3183 (2009)
7. Osman, Y.: Segmentation algorithm for Arabic handwritten text based on contour analysis. In: International Conference on Computing, Electrical and Electronics Engineering (ICCEEE), pp. 447–452. IEEE (2013)
8. Banumathi, K., Chandra, A.J.: Line and word segmentation of Kannada handwritten text documents using projection profile technique. In: International Conference on Electrical, Electronics, Communication, Computer and Optimization Techniques (ICEECCOT), pp. 196–201. IEEE (2016)
9. Khare, V., et al.: Weighted-gradient features for handwritten line segmentation. In: 24th International Conference on Pattern Recognition (ICPR), pp. 3651–3656. IEEE (2018)
10. Bouadjenek, N., Nemmour, H., Chibani, Y.: Age, gender and handedness prediction from handwriting using gradient features. In: 13th International Conference on Document Analysis and Recognition (ICDAR), pp. 1116–1120. IEEE (2015)
11. Maji, P., Chatterjee, S., Chakraborty, S., Kausar, N., Samanta, S., Dey, N.: Effect of Euler number as a feature in gender recognition system from offline handwritten signature using neural networks. In: 2nd International Conference on Computing for Sustainable Global Development (INDIACom), pp. 1869–1873. IEEE (2015)
12. Mirza, A., Moetesum, M., Siddiqi, I., Djeddi, C.: Gender classification from offline handwriting images using textural features. In: 15th International Conference on Frontiers in Handwriting Recognition (ICFHR), pp. 395–398. IEEE (2016)
13. Tan, J., Bi, N., Suen, C.Y., Nobile, N.: Multi-feature selection of handwriting for gender identification using mutual information. In: 15th International Conference on Frontiers in Handwriting Recognition (ICFHR), pp. 578–583. IEEE (2016)
14. Akbari, Y., Nouri, K., Sadri, J., Djeddi, C., Siddiqi, I.: Wavelet-based gender detection on off-line handwritten documents using probabilistic finite state automata. Image Vis. Comput. **59**, 17–30 (2017)
15. Navya, B., et al.: Adaptive multi-gradient kernels for handwritting based gender identification. In: 16th International Conference on Frontiers in Handwriting Recognition (ICFHR), pp. 392–397. IEEE (2018)

16. Moetesum, M., Siddiqi, I., Djeddi, C., Hannad, Y., Al-Maadeed, S.: Data driven feature extraction for gender classification using multi-script handwritten texts. In: 16th International Conference on Frontiers in Handwriting Recognition (ICFHR), pp. 564–569. IEEE (2018)
17. Saxena, A.K., Chaurasiya, V.K.: Multi-resolution texture analysis for fingerprint based age-group estimation. Multimedia Tools Appl. **77**(5), 6051–6077 (2018)
18. McAllister, P., Zheng, H., Bond, R., Moorhead, A.: Towards personalised training of machine learning algorithms for food image classification using a smartphone camera. In: García, C.R., Caballero-Gil, P., Burmester, M., Quesada-Arencibia, A. (eds.) UCAmI 2016. LNCS, vol. 10069, pp. 178–190. Springer, Cham (2016). https://doi.org/10.1007/978-3-319-48746-5_18

A Secure and Light Weight User Authentication System Based on Online Signature Verification for Resource Constrained Mobile Networks

Chandra Sekhar Vorugunti[1]([⊠]), D. S. Guru[2],
and Viswanath Pulabaigari[1]

[1] Indian Institute of Information Technology-SriCity, Chittoor, India
{chandrasekhar.v,viswanath.p}@iiits.in
[2] University of Mysore, Mysore, India
dsg@compsci.uni-mysore.ac.in

Abstract. The rapid advances in mobile and networking technologies results in usage of mobiles for critical applications like m-commerce, m-payments etc. Even though mobile based services offer many benefits, authenticating the user logging into the system is a big challenge. To mitigate this concern, secure mobile applications based on user online signature verification (OSV) has been proposed. Unfortunately, these models would intensify the substantial computational overhead on thin and resource-constrained mobile devices. This summarizes for a critical need of OSV models which are computationally efficient and achieves higher classification accuracy. Recently, several OSV models have been defined in the literature. However, these models are not computationally effective for resource-constrained mobile devices, because the proposed verification models ought to require not only higher feature dimension but also heavy weight writer specific parameter fixation logic. In this manuscript, we propose an efficient and light weight OSV model for resource-constrained mobile devices. Our approach employs dimensionality reduction based on DBSCAN clustering technique and user specific parameter selection. Thorough experimental analysis are conducted on benchmarking online signature datasets MCYT-100 (DB1) and MCYT-330 (DB2) datasets which confirms the efficiency of proposed model with latest OSV models.

Keywords: Mobile security · Dimensionality reduction ·
Online signature verification · Feature selection · Symbolic representation

1 Introduction

The technological progress observed over the past few decades coupled with the increasing accessibility of data, networks and other resources has led to new requirements for the securing of access to such resources.

Nowadays, the selection of the relevant access criteria are no longer based on the assumption that it is sufficient to verify a user's name and password, even if using a sophisticated encryption algorithm.

© Springer Nature Singapore Pte Ltd. 2019
S. Sundaram and G. Harit (Eds.): DAR 2018, CCIS 1020, pp. 133–140, 2019.
https://doi.org/10.1007/978-981-13-9361-7_12

Instead, modern security requirements and personal identification techniques are now being formulated on the basis of biometrics [3].

Biometrics is defined as those automated methods of personal identification and verification that are used for such a purpose and that are based on personal physiological features and the construction of the human body, or are based on specific behavioral features. Signature verification has remained one of the most widely accepted modalities to authenticate an individual primarily due to the ease with which signatures can be acquired. Being a behavioral biometric modality, the intra-personal variability in signatures is rather high and extremely unpredictable. This leads to relatively higher error rates as compared to those realized by other biometric traits like iris or fingerprints. Examples of physiological features include fingerprints and the structure of the retina or iris [1, 2]. Behavioral features include a handwritten signature, eye movement dynamics, the voice, and the dynamics of typing [11].

Among the various biometric methods, an approach based on handwritten signature recognition is one of the most popular [11, 16, 17, 20]. There are two approaches to the data collection component of a signature recognition process: dynamic and static. In the static method, a signature is recorded on paper and then converted into a digital form using a scanner [1, 11, 19]. This results in the shape of the signature being the only data source. The acquisition of dynamic features under the on-line mode is achieved by specialized devices, namely tablets [3, 11]. These devices, apart from capturing a signature images are capable inter alia of measuring position, inclination, velocity and the pressure placed on a pen as it marks out its successive points. The values of the features recorded across all of the individual discrete signature points can be presented in a numerical form. For example, at a given discrete signature point, a point's x, y pen coordinates, synthetic pen timestamps, penups, pen azimuth angle, altitude angle, and the pen pressure on the surface can be written as a set of values: (3172,6969, 63164065, 0, 1520, 450, 186).

In Song et al. [9], proposed an online signature verification based on extraction of stable features dynamically. Discriminative and effective signature features were extracted dynamically for each user. In order to extract spectral information based on simple and effective modified dynamic time warping (DTW) technique.

In Kar et al. [14], put forward an online signature verification in which signatures alignment and reference selection are an important task for signature verification. Due to inherent variability of the acquired signature, a novel technique called stroke point warping (SPW) is proposed.

In Xia et al. [11] proposed an OSV scheme based on selecting robust and discriminative features among the candidate signatures. To improve the robustness more consistent features are selected as candidates for discriminating the genuine and forgeries. In Zalasiński et al. [12], proposed a new signature partitioning technique which selects a unique partitions of signatures for each user separately. In the method proposed by Zalasiński et al. [12], the drive of this method is: (a) to intensify the accuracy of signature verification, (b) to eradicate the redundant segments, and (c) to shorten the verification of test signatures.

In Bouamra et al. [13], designed an effective offline signature verification system based on run-length distribution features. In Bouamra et al. [13] verification system, the model is trained with only the genuine signatures or positive specimens of each user and without any training with the forged samples. The classification of test sample is carried out using One-Class Support Vector Machine (OC-SVM)

The rapid advances in mobile and communication technologies result in usage of mobiles for critical applications like m-commerce, m-payments etc. The modern mobile gadgets like tablets, smart phones etc. allows users to access their critical data remotely by authenticating the user based on his/her online signature verification (OSV). Even though mobile based services offer many benefits, due to their inherent problems such as constrained battery life, storage and processing capacity, authenticating the user logging into the system is a big challenge and demands for light weight online signature verification models.

Online signature verification is a challenging task, due to the fact that the skilled forgeries and genuine handwritten signatures have intra-writer variability with close likenesses and distinctions. In order to reflect intra class variability, in literature [1–3, 5, 7], interval valued type data has been used to capture the intra class variability and thus have been capable of representing the real time scenarios.

In literature, several OSV models have been proposed by prioritizing various focus methods. Dynamic signature verification can be mainly categorize into feature-centric methods [1–3] which evaluate signatures grounded on a set of global or local features and function centric methods [6, 7] involve sequence matching techniques, such as Hidden Markov Models and DTW [17]. In literary texts, we can comprehend the implementation of different classifiers for online signature, such as interval valued classifier [1–3, 5], feature fusion based [3, 4], SVM [6], GMM [7], neural networks [3, 4], PCA [3], partition based [2], HMM [3, 4], distance or similarity based [1, 3, 5], fusion based classifier [4], stroke point warping-based reference selection [13], etc. In Doroz et al. [10] proposed an OSV based on a novel technique grounded on signature stability measure, grounded on fuzzy set theory. Signature stability measure is a biometric approach in which unstable fragments will not be taken into consideration while comparing the test signature samples with the reference set of signatures. The varying fragments among the reference signatures are termed as unstable fragments. Doroz et al. [10] method employs fuzzy sets to excerpt a signature's stable fragments. Li et al. [18] also proposed an OSV based on stable fragments of the signature. Alpar et al. [15] proposed an OSV based on continuous wavelet transformation of speed signals. Tang et al. [16] proposed an Information Divergence-Based Matching Strategy for Online Signature Verification. Napa et al. [19] proposed an OSV based on its distinctiveness, complexity, and repeatability of online signature templates.

However, these models are not computationally effective for resource-constrained mobile devices, because the adopted verification models should not only require higher feature dimension but also heavy weight writer specific parameter fixation logic.

2   Proposed Online Signature Verification Model

In this manuscript, to combat the above mentioned issues, we propose a verification model for online signature verification for resource constrained mobile networks based on dimensionality reduction using DBSCAN clustering and user specific parameters. The proposed model has four key stages namely:

1. Selection of user specific/dependent features based on feature relevance using DBSCAN clustering technique.
2. Representation of the user specific features in the form of an interval valued symbolic feature vector.
3. Fixing of user specific parameters, i.e. feature dimension and threshold using the logic described below.
4. Signature verification grounded on the user specific parameters. Steps A, B, C are one time activity for each user. Step D is executed in signature verification process, whenever user tries to log in to mobile network.

2.1 Selection of User Specific Features Based on Feature Relevance Using Feature Clustering Techniques

Let $S = [S_1^i, S_2^i, S_3^i, \ldots, S_n^i]$ be a set of 'n' signature samples of user 'i' i.e. U_i, i = 1, 2, 3,...N. (N represents the number of users). Let $F = [F_1^i, F_2^i, F_3^i, \ldots, F_m^i]$ be a set of m-dimensional combined feature vector, where $F_j^i = [f_{j1}^i, f_{j2}^i, f_{j3}^i, \ldots, f_{jn}^i]$ be the feature set characterizing the jth feature of signature samples of user 'i'. The Feature-Signature matrix (FS) of user U_i is shown below:

F/S	S_1	S_2	S_3		S_n
F_1	f_{11}	f_{12}			f_{1n}
F_2					
F_m	f_{m1}	f_{m2}			f_{mn}

To select the best 'd' discriminating features out of total 'm' features, we first clustered the features using the widely accepted density based clustering method DBSCAN, which is having inherent ability to determine the number of clusters into which the users feature vector can be clustered without the supplement of possible number of clusters as an input, which is not the case with widely used clustering techniques like K-NN, K-Means, K-Medoids etc.

Afterward, the cluster containing the maximum number of features is selected. The number of features in the larger cluster determines the user specific feature dimension and most discriminating features.

2.2 Representation of the User Specific Features in the Form of an Interval Valued Symbolic Feature Vector

As discussed above, to allow intra-user variability, for each user, the selected features are characterizes interval valued symbolic feature vector, e.g. the pth feature of the ith user i.e. f_{ip} is illustrated as $[f_{ip}^-, f_{ip}^+]$, in which f_{ip}^- and f_{ip}^+ denote the valid lower limit and the upper limit of f_{ip} and which are calculated as shown below:

$$f_{ip}^- = \text{Mean}(f_p^i) - \text{StdDev}(f_p^i) \tag{1}$$

and

$$f_{ip}^+ = \text{Mean}(f_p^i) - \text{StdDev}(f_p^i) \tag{2}$$

where Mean and StdDev corresponds to the mean and standard deviation of pth feature of the ith writer. In general, interval value representation of all of the 'd' features chosen for ith writer results in reference feature vector RFi, where

$$\text{RFi} = \left\{ \left[f_{i1}^-, f_{i1}^+ \right], \left[f_{i2}^-, f_{i2}^+ \right], \ldots, \left[f_{id}^-, f_{id}^+ \right] \right\} \tag{3}$$

The reference feature vector RF_i is stored in the knowledgebase corresponding to i^{th} writer and used in verification stage.

2.3 User Specific Parameter Fixation

Once the discriminative features are selected and represented as reference feature vector, as shown below, for each user, twenty trials have been taken by varying the threshold similarity from 0.1 to 0.9 in steps of 0.1. to select the best threshold which results in lowest EER.

Logic for writer specific parameter fixation i.e. similarity threshold.
for iUser = 1: 100
Cluster the iUser features using DBSCAN clustering algorithm.
// The cluster with larger features is selected and the number of features in the larger
// cluster is the iUser feature dimension.
for trialno = 1:20
for Threshold = 0.1 : 0.9
// Compute the FAR: False Acceptance Ratio, FRR: False Reject Ratio, EER : Equal Error Rate
end
end
end // end of for iUser.
// The threshold which results min EER is assigned to i^{th} User.

The False Reject Ratio – FRR (the number of genuine signatures rejected as forgery out of total genuine signatures tested) and False Acceptance Ratio–FAR (the number of forgery signatures accepted as genuine out of total number forgery samples) are computed. Finally, Equal Error Rate - ERR (the point at which the FAR equal to FRR) is calculated from the receiver operating characteristics (ROC) curves. The combination of feature indices, feature dimension, threshold which results in minimum EER are fixed as parameters for each writer. Once the parameters are fixed, for any verification task, the fixed parameters are retrieved from knowledge base and used in verification task as discussed below.

2.4   Signature Verification Based on the Writer Specific Parameters

On receiving the test signature Tests from user U_j for verification, represented by its 'm' dimensional feature vector say FTest = $\{f_{t1}, f_{t2}, ..., f_{tm}\}$, to qualify its genuineness, the user specific parameters are retrieved from the knowledge base. The crisp values of writer specific features i.e. f_{t1}, f_{t2} etc. of test signature are compared with the corresponding symbolic reference feature vector of the claimed user i.e. $RF_i = $. If the number of features of test signature which falls in the valid range of their corresponding symbolic reference feature vector are greater than or equal to his similarity threshold, the signature is qualified as genuine else it is forgery.

3   Experimentation and Results

Dataset: To verify the efficiency of our proposed model, we have conducted experiments on widely used MCYT-100 (DB1) dataset [3, 4] which contains 25 genuine and 25 skilled forgeries for 100 users and 100 global features for each online signature. Table 1, illustrates the experimental results of the proposed model with MCYT-330 dataset, Due to unavailability of models experimented with MCYT-330 dataset, we are unable to compare our work with other proposed models.

Table 1. Comparative analysis of the proposed model against the contemporary models on MCYT (DB2) database

Method	S_05	S_20	R_05	R_20
Proposed: DBSCAN based clustering with symbolic representation of writer dependent parameters	9.67	7.71	4.27	2.01

Table 2 illustrates the performance of various signature verification systems based on DB1 dataset. Details of some of the above mentioned models can be found in [1–4]. From Table 2, it is affirm that our proposed model is efficient compared to many recently proposed models like writer dependent features [1, 2, 4, 5], Base classifier (BASE), Nearest neighbor description (NND) etc.

Although the EER our model realized is slightly high in case of skilled_05, due to the fact that, our model fixed very few features e.g. 28 for writer 18, 44 etc. as depicted in Table 2, whereas [1, 2, 4, 5] etc. used minimum 50 features in case of skilled_20 and random_20 categories and 60 features in case of skilled_05 and random_05 categories, while other models [3, 7, 8] used entire 100 global features. Reduced feature set dimension makes our verification model light weight and realistic.

Table 2. Comparative analysis of the proposed model against the contemporary models on MCYT (DB1) database

Method	S_05	S_20	R_05	R_20
Proposed: DBSCAN based clustering with symbolic representation of writer dependent parameters	11.67	8.89	5.89	2.32
Writer dependent features based on spectral clustering [1]	14.9	5.0	7.9	2.0
Writer dependent features and classifiers [2]	19.4	1.1	7.8	0.8
Regularized Parzen window classifier RPWC [3]	9.7	-	3.4	-
Symbolic classifier [1]	15.4	4.2	3.6	1.2
Fusion methods [3]	7.6	-	2.3	-
Gaussian model description [2]	7.7	4.4	5.1	1.5
Support vector description (SVD) [2]	8.9	5.4	3.8	1.6
Ensemble of one class classifier based on over completer feature generation [4]	4.5	2.2	1.5	0.5
Random ensemble of base (RS) [3]	9.0	-	5.3	-
Principal component analysis description (PCAD) [2]	7.9	4.2	3.8	1.4
Parzen window classifier (PWC) [2]	9.7	5.2	3.4	1.4
User dependent features [5]	14.9	5.0	7.9	2.2
Ensemble of Parzen window classifier [7]	8.4	-	2.9	-
Base classifier (BASE) [3]	17.0	-	8.3	-
Mixture of Gaussian description_3(MOGD_3) [2]	8.9	7.3	5.4	4.3
Mixture of Gaussian description_2 (MOGD_2) [2]	8.1	7.0	5.4	4.3
Kholmatov model (KHA) [3]	11.3	-	5.8	-
Nearest neighbor description (NND) [2]	12.2	6.3	6.9	2.1
Linear programing description (LPD) [2]	9.4	5.6	3.6	2.5
Cluster dependent classifiers for online signature verification [8]	12.6	1.0	6.5	0.4
Random subspace ensemble with resampling of base (RSB) [3]	9.0	-	5.0	-
Cluster based symbolic representation [2]	15.4	4.2	3.6	1.2
Signature partitioning [9]	-	-	5.28	4.48
Enhanced DTW + DTW [17]	-	-	3.76	
Enhanced DTW [17]	-	-	2.66	

4   Conclusion and Future Work

In this work, we put forward a novel, light weight online signature verification model for resource constrained mobile networks grounded on writer specific feature clustering based on DBSCAN and interval-valued representation of feature values. The proposed model has been thoroughly tested using widely accepted MCYT-100 and MCYT-330 datasets. The experimental outcomes summarize that the proposed model achieved best results compared to the latest literature.

References

1. Guru, D.S., Manjunatha, K.S., Manjunath, S.: User dependent features in online signature verification. In: Swamy, P., Guru, D. (eds.) Multimedia Processing, Communication and Computing Applications. Lecture Notes in Electrical Engineering, pp. 229–240. Springer, New Delhi (2013). https://doi.org/10.1007/978-81-322-1143-3_19
2. Manjunath, S., Manjunatha, K.S., Guru, D.S., Somashekara, M.T.: Cluster dependent classifiers for online signature verification. In: Prasath, R., Vuppala, A.K., Kathirvalavakumar, T. (eds.) MIKE 2015. LNCS (LNAI), vol. 9468, pp. 58–69. Springer, Cham (2015). https://doi.org/10.1007/978-3-319-26832-3_7
3. Cpałka, K., Zalasiński, M., Rutkowski, L.: New method for the on-line signature verification based on horizontal partitioning. J. Pattern Recognit. **47**, 2652–2661 (2014)
4. Manjunatha, K.S., Manjunath, S., Guru, D.S., Somashekara, M.T.: Online signature verification based on writer dependent features and classifiers. Pattern Recogn. Lett. **80**, 129–136 (2016)
5. Guru, D.S., Manjunatha, K.S., Manjunath, S., Somashekara, M.T.: Interval valued symbolic representation of writer dependent features for online signature verification. J. Expert Syst. Appl. **80**, 232–243 (2017)
6. Alaei, A., Pal, S., Pal, S., Blumenstein, M.: An efficient signature verification method based on an interval symbolic representation and a fuzzy similarity measure. IEEE Trans. Inf. Forensics Secur. **12** (2017)
7. Rohilla, S., Sharma, A.: Online signature verification technique using reference feature vector. Proc. Natl. Acad. Sci. India Sect. A **87**, 125 (2017)
8. Xia, X., Chen, Z., Luan, F., Song, X.: Signature alignment based on GMM for on-line signature verification. J. Pattern Recogn. **65**, 188–196 (2017)
9. Song, X., Xia, X., Luan, F.: Online signature verification based on stable features extracted dynamically. IEEE Trans. Syst. Man Cybern. Syst. **47** (2017)
10. Doroz, R., Kudlacik, P., Porwik, P.: Online signature verification modeled by stability-oriented reference signatures. Inf. Sci. **460–461**, 151–171 (2018)
11. Xia, X., Song, X., Luan, F., Zheng, J., Chen, Z., Ma, X.: Discriminative feature selection for on-line signature verification. J. Pattern Recogn. **74**, 422–433 (2018)
12. Marcin, Z., Krzysztof, C.: A new method for signature verification based on selection of the most important partitions of the dynamic signature. J. Neuro Comput. **289**, 13–22 (2018)
13. Bouamra, W., Djeddi, C., Nini, B., Diaz, M., Siddiqi, I.: Towards the design of an offline signature verifier based on a small number of genuine samples for training. J. Expert Syst. Appl. **107**, 182–195 (2018)
14. Kar, B., Mukherjee, A., Dutta, P.K.: Stroke point warping-based reference selection and verification of online signature. IEEE Trans. Instrum. Meas. **67**, 2–11 (2018)
15. Alpar, O.: Online signature verification by continuous wavelet transformation of speed signals. Expert Syst. Appl. **104**, 33–42 (2018)
16. Tang, L., Kang, W., Fang, Y.: Information divergence-based matching strategy for online signature verification. IEEE Trans. Inf. Forensics Secur. **13** (2018)
17. Abhishek, S., Suresh, S.: On the exploration of information from the DTW cost matrix for online signature verification. IEEE Trans. Cybern. **48**, 611–624 (2018)
18. Li, Y., Xiaoyan, J., Qi, J.: Online handwritten signature verification based on the most stable feature and partition. J. Cluster Comput. **6**, 1–11 (2018)
19. Napa, S., Nasir, M., Pitikhate, S.: Distinctiveness, complexity, and repeatability of online signature templates. Pattern Recogn. **84**, 332–344 (2018)
20. Zalasińskia, M., Cpałkaa, K.: A new method for signature verification based on selection of the most important partitions of the dynamic signature. J. Neurocomput. **289**, 13–22 (2018)

Datasets and Performance Evaluation

Benchmark Datasets for Offline Handwritten Gurmukhi Script Recognition

Munish Kumar[1(✉)], R. K. Sharma[2], M. K. Jindal[3],
Simpel Rani Jindal[4], and Harjeet Singh[2]

[1] Department of Computational Sciences, Maharaja Ranjit Singh Punjab
Technical University, Bathinda, Punjab, India
munishcse@gmail.com

[2] Computer Science and Engineering Department,
Thapar Institute of Engineering and Technology, Patiala, Punjab, India
{rksharma, harjeet.singh}@thapar.edu

[3] Department of Computer Science and Applications,
Panjab University Regional Centre, Muktsar, Punjab, India
manishphd@rediffmail.com

[4] Department of Computer Science and Engineering,
Yadavindra College of Engineering, Talwandi Sabo, Bathinda, Punjab, India
simpel_jindal@rediffmail.com

Abstract. Handwritten character recognition is an imperative issue in the field of pattern recognition and machine learning research. In the recent years, several techniques for handwritten character recognition have been proposed. Due to the lack of publicly accessible benchmark datasets of Gurmukhi script, no extensive comparisons have been undertaken between those techniques, especially for this script. Over the years, datasets and benchmarks have proven their fundamental importance in character recognition research, and objective comparisons in many fields. This paper presents a collection of seven benchmark datasets (HWR-Gurmukhi_1.1, HWR-Gurmukhi_1.2, HWR-Gurmukhi_1.3, HWR-Gurmukhi_2.1, HWR-Gurmukhi_2.2, HWR-Gurmukhi_2.3, and HWR-Gurmukhi_3.1) with different sizes for offline handwritten Gurmukhi character recognition collected from various public places. A few exploratory outcomes based on precision, False Acceptance Rate (FAR), and False Rejection Rate (FRR) using different classification techniques, namely, k-NN, RBF-SVM, MLP, Neural Network, Decision Tree, and Random Forest are also presented in this paper.

Keywords: Handwritten character recognition · Gurmukhi dataset ·
Benchmarking · Classification

1 Introduction

Document Analysis and Recognition (DAR) systems play a major role in data transfer between human beings and computers. Optical Character Recognition (OCR) system is an essential part of a document analysis and recognition system. In the recent years, applying machine learning techniques in the field of optical character recognition have

© Springer Nature Singapore Pte Ltd. 2019
S. Sundaram and G. Harit (Eds.): DAR 2018, CCIS 1020, pp. 143–151, 2019.
https://doi.org/10.1007/978-981-13-9361-7_13

drawn a lot of attention. Offline Handwritten Character Recognition system, commonly abbreviated as offline HCR, is the process of converting offline handwritten text into a format that is understood by machine. It involves processing of documents containing scanned images of a text written by a user, generally on a sheet of paper. Many techniques have been presented for offline handwritten character recognition. These techniques are tested on a handful of specific datasets. But, systematic comparisons of these techniques are not available due to the lack of benchmark datasets for Gurmukhi characters. In this paper, we introduce a collection of datasets for benchmarking the character recognition techniques.

There are seven types (HWR-Gurmukhi_1.1, HWR-Gurmukhi_1.2, HWR-Gurmukhi_1.3, HWR-Gurmukhi_2.1, HWR-Gurmukhi_2.2, HWR-Gurmukhi_2.3, and HWR-Gurmukhi_3.1) of benchmark datasets as presented in Table 1. All the images in these datasets are normalized to the size 100×100. Along these lines, the dimensionality of every test image vector is $10,000$ ($=100 \times 100$), where every component is binary. These datasets can be used to conduct quantitative performance testing and systematic comparisons of approaches, and will also be helpful for determining the statistical significance of the findings. Finally, we have created a web page that contains benchmark datasets of Gurmukhi characters and provide a resource to the scientific community for development of new alignment and inference methods. All the resources of these benchmark datasets have been made publicly available at https://sites.google.com/view/gurmukhi-benchmark/.

2 Related Work

Many researchers have worked on character and numeral recognition in last couple of years. Djeddi et al. [1] have presented a work in ICFHR2016 competition on multi-script writer demographics classification using "QUWI" database. QUWI is a bilingual database which contains writing samples of same individuals in Arabic and English. The competition was aimed at reporting and comparing the latest techniques on these problems under the same experimental settings. Xing and Qiao [2] have proposed a text independent approach to identify the writer for offline handwritten images. In order to extract discriminative features, they employed a deep Convolutional Neural Network (CNN). Experiments are evaluated on two datasets, namely, IAM dataset containing handwritten English text and HWDB dataset containing handwritten Chinese text.

Kumar et al. [3] have presented efficient feature extraction techniques for offline handwritten Gurmukhi character recognition. They have also presented a hierarchical technique for offline handwritten Gurmukhi character recognition [4]. Recent survey on the character and numeral recognition has been presented by Kumar et al. [5]. They organized the survey in several ways, i.e., recognition results using script wise, feature extraction technique wise, etc. They also observed that various techniques have been presented for offline handwritten Gurmukhi character recognition, but comparisons of results are not presented due to the lack of public Gurmukhi script dataset. Furthermore, there are some challenges in handwriting recognition like writer dependency or independency. So, we have presented different types of datasets as presented in Table 1. Detailed description about each dataset is given in next section.

Table 1. Gurmukhi datasets

Dataset	Number of writers	Number of samples per class	Number of classes	Number of training samples	Number of testing samples	Total samples
HWR-Gurmukhi_1.1	1	100	35	2450	1050	3500
HWR-Gurmukhi_1.2	10	10	35	2450	1050	3500
HWR-Gurmukhi_1.3	100	1	35	2450	1050	3500
HWR-Gurmukhi_2.1	1	100	56	3920	1680	5600
HWR-Gurmukhi_2.2	10	10	56	3920	1680	5600
HWR-Gurmukhi_2.3	100	1	56	3920	1680	5600
HWR-Gurmukhi_3.1	200	1	35	4900	2100	7000

3 Gurmukhi Script and Description of Data Set

Gurmukhi script has 35 fundamental characters (three vowel bearers and thirty-two consonants) and 21 additional characters. These 21 characters are: six additional consonants, nine vowel modifiers, three auxiliary signs, and three half characters. Our dataset collection has seven categories:

(i)   HWR-Gurmukhi_1.1,
(ii) HWR-Gurmukhi_1.2,
(iii) HWR-Gurmukhi_1.3,
(iv) HWR-Gurmukhi_2.1,
(v)   HWR-Gurmukhi_2.2,
(vi) HWR-Gurmukhi_2.3, and
(vii) HWR-Gurmukhi_3.1

Category HWR-Gurmukhi_1.1 consists of one hundred samples each of 35 fundamental offline handwritten Gurmukhi characters where each Gurmukhi character is written by a single writer. Category HWR-Gurmukhi_1.2 consists of one hundred samples each of 35 fundamental offline handwritten Gurmukhi characters where each Gurmukhi character is written ten times by ten different writers. In Category HWR-Gurmukhi_1.3, each fundamental Gurmukhi character is written once by one hundred different writers. Total number of samples are 3500 in each of the datasets HWR-Gurmukhi_1.1, HWR-Gurmukhi_1.2, and HWR-Gurmukhi_1.3.

The dataset HWR-Gurmukhi_2.1 consists of one hundred samples of all 56 offline handwritten Gurmukhi characters where each Gurmukhi character is written by a single writer. The dataset HWR-Gurmukhi_2.2, consists of one hundred samples of all offline handwritten Gurmukhi characters where each Gurmukhi character is written ten times by ten different writers. In dataset HWR-Gurmukhi_2.3, each Gurmukhi character is written once by one hundred different writers. The datasets in each category are also partitioned into training dataset (70% samples) and testing dataset (30% samples). This can further be experimented by a potential user of these datasets.

4   Evaluation of Existing Techniques Using Benchmark Datasets

Various feature extraction techniques and classification techniques have been used for character recognition, but it is difficult to evaluate the relative performance of a novel algorithm due to the non-availability of benchmark dataset. This section illustrates a comparative study of some existing features and classification techniques using the collection of benchmark datasets (HWR-Gurmukhi_1.1, HWR-Gurmukhi_1.2, HWR-Gurmukhi_1.3, HWR-Gurmukhi_2.1, HWR-Gurmukhi_2.2, HWR-Gurmukhi_2.3, and HWR-Gurmukhi_3.1) considered in this paper.

A total of 6 feature extraction techniques and 6 classification techniques are evaluated in this paper based on Precision rate, False Acceptance Rate (FAR), and False Rejection Rate (FRR). Feature extraction techniques include zoning features, diagonal features, intersection and open end points, directional features, transition features, and centroid features. Classification techniques evaluated for these benchmark datasets are k-NN, RBF-SVM, MLP, Decision Tree, and Random Forest. Precision rate, True Positive Rate (TPR), and False Positive Rate (FPR) of all benchmark datasets are depicted in Table 2, 3 and 4, respectively.

Table 2. Precision rate of Gurmuskhi benchmark datasets

Data set	Classifier	Zoning features	Diagonal features	Intersection and open end points features	Directional features	Transitions features	Centroid features
HWR-Gurmukhi_1.1	k-NN	94.9%	95.1%	95.0%	86.9%	90.7%	95.6%
	RBF-SVM	93.7%	93.7%	94.8%	86.8%	90.2%	91.0%
	MLP	96.4%	96.6%	96.5%	91.7%	94.9%	96.8%
	Decision tree	81.8%	81.9%	82.1%	71.0%	82.3%	82.9%
	Random forest	97.1%	97.4%	97.0%	93.7%	91.3%	96.6%
HWR-Gurmukhi_1.2	k-NN	88.4%	88.4%	88.4%	79.3%	80.6%	90.4%
	RBF-SVM	78.6%	78.6%	83.3%	57.4%	73.4%	75.6%
	MLP	91.6%	91.6%	92.2%	73.5%	85.0%	90.3%
	Decision tree	73.8%	73.2%	71.1%	64.0%	71.1%	72.3%
	Random forest	93.4%	93.1%	93.5%	80.9%	89.4%	93.0%

(continued)

Table 2. (*continued*)

Data set	Classifier	Zoning features	Diagonal features	Intersection and open end points features	Directional features	Transitions features	Centroid features
HWR-Gurmukhi_1.3	k-NN	81.6%	81.6%	79.7%	66.5%	73.8%	81.3%
	RBF-SVM	74.8%	74.8%	79.2%	49.6%	66.7%	70.4%
	MLP	83.5%	83.2%	85.1%	91.7%	78.9%	81.6%
	Decision tree	56.7%	56.7%	55.7%	43.6%	57.7%	56.8%
	Random forest	86.7%	70.8%	87.6%	67.2%	84.1%	86.9%
HWR-Gurmukhi_2.1	k-NN	90.8%	90.8%	90.8%	79.0%	85.7%	88.3%
	RBF-SVM	84.4%	84.5%	85.0%	68.6%	77.0%	81.2%
	MLP	90.6%	90.9%	91.1%	81.3%	87.4%	90.2%
	Decision tree	74.4%	74.2%	71.6%	63.5%	75.1%	73.1%
	Random forest	92.2%	92.6%	92.0%	87.8%	92.1%	92.2%
HWR-Gurmukhi_2.2	k-NN	86.2%	86.3%	87.7%	80.4%	81.0%	85.9%
	RBF-SVM	67.6%	67.8%	72.8%	45.2%	54.1%	65.9%
	MLP	91.5%	81.8%	85.4%	67.1%	78.3%	83.4%
	Decision tree	69.9%	69.9%	66.6%	59.2%	69.8%	68.5%
	Random forest	90.4%	87.5%	88.4%	81.8%	86.9%	88.2%
HWR-Gurmukhi_2.3	k-NN	81.9%	81.8%	83.5%	70.4%	74.2%	80.2%
	RBF-SVM	65.8%	65.7%	70.4%	34.1%	52.8%	64.0%
	MLP	77.5%	77.3%	83.4%	59.3%	71.8%	79.1%
	Decision tree	61.7%	61.7%	59.3%	49.5%	60.1%	58.1%
	Random forest	83.9%	84.4%	85.3%	77.6%	84.5%	83.4%
HWR-Gurmukhi_3.1	k-NN	84.4%	84.4%	84.7%	72.5%	74.9%	85.2%
	RBF-SVM	79.6%	79.6%	81.3%	57.5%	67.8%	73.9%
	MLP	85.1%	85.1%	87.3%	61.3%	78.6%	85.3%
	Decision tree	65.3%	65.3%	64.0%	52.8%	66.4%	66.8%
	Random forest	90.4%	90.5%	89.3%	72.4%	83.2%	89.8%

Table 3. True Positive Rate (TPR) of Gurmukhi benchmark datasets

Data set	Classifier	Zoning features	Diagonal features	Intersection and open end points features	Directional features	Transitions features	Centroid features
HWR-Gurmukhi_1.1	k-NN	94.8%	95.0%	94.6%	84.1%	89.4%	95.4%
	RBF-SVM	93.2%	93.2%	94.5%	85.8%	86.5%	90.8%
	MLP	96.2%	96.4%	96.3%	91.3%	94.4%	96.7%
	Decision tree	81.2%	81.3%	81.2%	70.1%	81.7%	82.2%
	Random forest	97.0%	97.2%	96.9%	93.4%	90.4%	96.5%
HWR-Gurmukhi_1.2	k-NN	87.6%	91.2%	87.6%	74.5%	79.3%	89.7%
	RBF-SVM	75.6%	75.6%	82.0%	52.1%	62.1%	72.9%
	MLP	91.2%	91.2%	91.9%	73.0%	84.7%	90.1%
	Decision tree	72.5%	72.1%	69.8%	62.1%	70.0%	71.5%
	Random forest	93.1%	92.9%	93.2%	80.5%	89.0%	92.8%
HWR-Gurmukhi_1.3	k-NN	80.3%	80.3%	78.4%	59.7%	71.5%	79.7%
	RBF-SVM	71.9%	71.9%	76.6%	39.2%	61.6%	65.9%
	MLP	82.7%	82.4%	84.5%	91.3%	78.2%	80.8%
	Decision tree	55.3%	55.3%	54.3%	42.5%	56.6%	55.7%
	Random forest	86.1%	68.4%	87.0%	66.0%	82.8%	86.1%
HWR-Gurmukhi_2.1	k-NN	89.8%	89.8%	89.9%	75.9%	84.7%	87.4%
	RBF-SVM	79.8%	79.8%	82.1%	66.8%	73.2%	78.1%
	MLP	89.9%	90.4%	90.7%	80.8%	87.0%	89.8%
	Decision tree	73.0%	72.7%	69.6%	61.6%	74.0%	72.1%
	Random forest	91.6%	91.8%	91.5%	87.3%	91.7%	91.7%
HWR-Gurmukhi_2.2	k-NN	85.4%	85.4%	86.9%	76.5%	79.9%	84.9%
	RBF-SVM	64.2%	64.5%	69.1%	37.9%	50.2%	61.1%
	MLP	91.1%	81.3%	84.6%	66.7%	77.7%	83.1%
	Decision tree	68.5%	68.5%	65.4%	58.5%	68.9%	67.7%
	Random forest	90.2%	86.7%	87.8%	81.1%	86.4%	87.6%

(continued)

Table 3. (*continued*)

Data set	Classifier	Zoning features	Diagonal features	Intersection and open end points features	Directional features	Transitions features	Centroid features
HWR-Gurmukhi_2.3	k-NN	80.5%	80.4%	82.4%	65.5%	72.6%	79.2%
	RBF-SVM	61.0%	60.9%	65.9%	30.2%	48.5%	57.7%
	MLP	76.7%	76.5%	82.7%	58.5%	70.5%	78.5%
	Decision tree	59.9%	59.9%	58.0%	48.8%	58.3%	57.4%
	Random forest	83.1%	83.4%	84.6%	76.1%	83.8%	82.5%
HWR-Gurmukhi_3.1	k-NN	83.6%	83.6%	84.0%	66.5%	73.5%	84.6%
	RBF-SVM	78.6%	78.6%	80.4%	55.4%	66.0%	72.8%
	MLP	84.9%	84.9%	87.0%	61.0%	78.7%	85.0%
	Decision tree	64.4%	64.4%	63.1%	52.2%	65.7%	65.9%
	Random forest	90.1%	90.3%	89.0%	71.0%	82.9%	89.6%

Table 4. False Positive Rate (FPR) of Gurmukhi benchmark datasets

Data set	Classifier	Zoning features	Diagonal features	Intersection and open end points features	Directional features	Transitions features	Centroid features
HWR-Gurmukhi_1.1	k-NN	0.1%	0.1%	0.2%	0.4%	0.3%	0.1%
	RBF-SVM	0.2%	0.2%	0.2%	0.4%	0.3%	0.3%
	MLP	0.1%	0.3%	0.1%	0.2%	0.2%	0.1%
	Decision tree	0.6%	0.6%	0.6%	0.9%	0.5%	0.5%
	Random forest	0.1%	0.1%	0.1%	0.2%	0.3%	0.1%
HWR-Gurmukhi_1.2	k-NN	0.4%	0.4%	0.4%	0.7%	0.6%	0.3%
	RBF-SVM	0.7%	0.7%	0.5%	1.3%	1.0%	0.8%
	MLP	0.3%	0.3%	0.2%	0.8%	0.4%	0.3%
	Decision tree	0.8%	0.8%	0.9%	1.1%	0.9%	0.8%
	Random forest	0.2%	0.2%	0.2%	0.6%	0.3%	0.2%
HWR-Gurmukhi_1.3	k-NN	0.6%	0.6%	0.6%	1.1%	0.8%	0.6%
	RBF-SVM	0.8%	0.8%	0.7%	1.6%	1.1%	1.0%
	MLP	0.5%	0.5%	0.4%	0.2%	0.6%	0.6%
	Decision tree	1.3%	1.3%	1.3%	1.7%	1.3%	1.3%
	Random forest	0.4%	0.9%	0.4%	1.0%	0.5%	0.4%

(*continued*)

Table 4. (*continued*)

Data set	Classifier	Zoning features	Diagonal features	Intersection and open end points features	Directional features	Transitions features	Centroid features
HWR-Gurmukhi_2.1	k-NN	0.2%	0.2%	0.2%	0.4%	0.3%	0.2%
	RBF-SVM	0.3%	0.3%	0.3%	0.6%	0.5%	0.4%
	MLP	0.2%	0.2%	0.2%	0.4%	0.2%	0.2%
	Decision tree	0.5%	0.5%	0.5%	0.7%	0.5%	0.5%
	Random forest	0.2%	0.1%	0.2%	0.2%	0.2%	0.1%
HWR-Gurmukhi_2.2	k-NN	0.3%	0.3%	0.2%	0.4%	0.4%	0.3%
	RBF-SVM	0.6%	0.6%	0.5%	1.0%	0.8%	0.7%
	MLP	0.3%	0.3%	0.3%	0.6%	0.4%	0.3%
	Decision tree	0.6%	0.6%	0.6%	0.8%	0.6%	0.6%
	Random forest	0.3%	0.2%	0.2%	0.3%	0.2%	0.2%
HWR-Gurmukhi_2.3	k-NN	0.3%	0.4%	0.3%	0.6%	0.5%	0.4%
	RBF-SVM	0.7%	0.7%	0.6%	1.1%	0.9%	0.7%
	MLP	0.4%	0.4%	0.3%	0.8%	0.5%	0.4%
	Decision tree	0.7%	0.7%	0.8%	0.9%	0.7%	0.8%
	Random forest	0.3%	0.3%	0.3%	0.4%	0.3%	0.3%
HWR-Gurmukhi_3.1	k-NN	0.5%	0.5%	0.5%	1.0%	0.8%	0.4%
	RBF-SVM	0.6%	0.6%	0.6%	1.3%	1.0%	0.8%
	MLP	0.4%	0.4%	0.4%	1.1%	0.6%	0.4%
	Decision tree	0.1%	0.1%	1.1%	1.4%	1.0%	1.0%
	Random forest	0.3%	0.3%	0.3%	0.8%	0.5%	0.3%

5   Conclusion

In this paper, we have introduced a collection of seven benchmark datasets for offline handwritten Gurmukhi character recognition. We hope that publication of these benchmark datasets will facilitate research for offline handwritten Gurmukhi script. These datasets would help in comparing the existing techniques and proposed techniques by various researchers in future. We plan to enrich these datasets in future by adding more samples and also by inviting researchers to contribute. Enriching the datasets will be an interesting and challenging future work.

Conflict of Interest. The authors declare that they have no conflict of interest.

References

1. Djeddi, C., Al-Maadeed, S., Gattal, A., Siddiqi, I., Ennaji, A., Abed, H.E.: ICFHR2016 competition on multi-script writer demographics classification using "QUWI" database. In: Proceedings of the 15th International Conference on Frontiers in Handwriting Recognition, pp. 602–606 (2016)
2. Xing, L., Qiao, Y.: DeepWriter: a multi-stream deep CNN for text-independent writer identification. In: Proceedings of the 15th International Conference on Frontiers in Handwriting Recognition, pp. 584–589 (2016)
3. Kumar, M., Sharma, R.K., Jindal, M.K.: Efficient feature extraction techniques for offline handwritten gurmukhi character recognition. Natl. Acad. Sci. Lett. **37**(4), 381–391 (2014)
4. Kumar, M., Jindal, M.K., Sharma, R.K.: A novel hierarchical technique for offline handwritten gurmukhi character recognition. Natl. Acad. Sci. Lett. **37**(6), 567–572 (2014)
5. Kumar, M., Sharma, R.K., Jindal, M.K., Jindal, S.R.: Character recognition for non-indic and indic scripts: a literature survey. Artif. Intell. Rev. (2018). https://doi.org/10.1007/s10462-017-9607-x

Benchmark Dataset: Offline Handwritten Gurmukhi City Names for Postal Automation

Harmandeep Kaur and Munish Kumar[⊠]

Department of Computational Sciences, Maharaja Ranjit Singh
Punjab Technical University, Bathinda, Punjab, India
harmandeepk08@gmail.com, munishcse@gmail.com

Abstract. Handwriting recognition delineate the computer's ability to convert human handwriting into text that can be processed by machine. Postal automation plays a significant role in image processing and pattern recognition field. Handwritten city name recognition is the part of postal automation. For assessing the performance of the existing techniques for handwritten city name recognition, a standardized dataset proves useful. But due to lack of publicly accessible benchmark dataset in Gurmukhi script, a systematic comparison of the existing techniques for Gurmukhi city name recognition is not feasible. In this paper, we have presented a dataset for Gurmukhi postal automation named as HWR-Gurmukhi_Postal_1.0 which contains total 40,000 samples of names of various cities which are written in Gurmukhi script. This dataset can be seen as a benchmark for comparison among existing techniques for handwritten city name recognition.

Keywords: Postal automation · Gurmukhi words · City names ·
Gurmukhi dataset · Benchmarking

1 Introduction

At present, many paper documents are converted into electronic form that makes it easy to process information. Researchers proved that the identification of both barcodes and printed text through Optical Character Recognition (OCR) is reliable and significantly accelerates data processing. OCR can be defined as the process of transforming scanned images of typed, printed or handwritten text into machine form, either in the form of plain text or a word document that can be interpreted by the computer. Recognition of Offline handwritten documents is an imperative domain in the pattern recognition field. Offline Handwritten Word Recognition (HWR) principally entails OCR and finds its real world applications in many areas, which make it a prospective dominant research field in document analysis and recognition. Offline HWR recognizes words after it was written on paper and extract the information about these words from a digitized image. It comprises documents processing that contains scanned images of handwritten text on paper sheets. In Offline HWR, two dimensional images are acquired after digitization.

There are mainly two approaches to recognition of handwritten words, namely, analytical approach and a holistic approach. An analytical approach is also known as

© Springer Nature Singapore Pte Ltd. 2019
S. Sundaram and G. Harit (Eds.): DAR 2018, CCIS 1020, pp. 152–159, 2019.
https://doi.org/10.1007/978-981-13-9361-7_14

segmentation based approach, where words are not considered as an individual entity, rather it comprises smaller size units called characters. At first the words are partitioned into the characters and then for the recognition purpose, character model is employed. In a holistic approach, the word itself is considered as an individual entity and thus recognition is globally performed on the whole word without dividing it into characters. The holistic method is free from explicit segmentation and thus also known as a segmentation free approach. Many techniques have been presented for offline HWR, but due to lack of benchmark dataset for Gurmukhi script, systematic comparisons of these techniques are not available.

In this paper, we have introduced a dataset for a benchmarking postal automation of Gurmukhi script. There are 100 classes of benchmark dataset. The proposed dataset will be helpful for making comparisons among existing techniques for handwritten city name recognition and also for determining the statistical significance of the findings. Now, https://sites.google.com/view/gurmukhi-benchmark/home/word-level-gurmukhi-dataset link has been made publicly for HWR-Gurmukhi_Postal_1.0 dataset.

2   Related Work

Various benchmark datasets have been created by researchers and enough work has been done in the area of word recognition. For example, Mahadevan and Srihari [1] presented an approach to parsing and recognition of city, state and ZIP codes in handwritten addresses. For evaluation, they have considered a database of 76,121 entries of city, state and ZIP codes and it has been concluded that in 75% of the cases, the correct entry is set to rank of at most 10. Liu et al. [2] have developed a lexicon driven segmentation and recognition system for handwritten character strings in order to read Japanese addresses. The proposed method is evaluated on 3,589 live mail images with 83.68% correct rate by considering the error rate less than 1%. Alaei et al. [3] have presented Kannada Handwritten Text Database (KHTD) which contains 204 handwritten documents written by 51 writers. The database contains 4298 text-lines and 26115 words. On the basis of pixel's information and content information, two kinds of ground truths are produced for the database. Pal et al. [4] proposed a lexicon driven method for recognition of city names handwritten in Bangla script for postal automation using Modified Quadratic Discriminant Function (MQDF). Experiments are conducted on dataset comprising 84 city names handwritten in Bangla script which reported 94.08% accuracy. They have also proposed lexicon driven approach for recognizing city names handwritten in three languages like Hindi, Bangla and English language [5]. This is the first work of its kind that deals with recognition of tri-lingual city names. They tested the proposed approach on dataset comprising 16,132 Indian city names written in three languages and reported a recognition accuracy of 92.25%.

Rani et al. [6] presented Gabor filters feature extraction method that is based on zone approach for recognition of Gurmukhi and English scripts at the level of word. They have experimented the approach on dataset of 11,400 words comprising 5212 Gurmukhi words, 4288 English words and 1900 English numerals and finally reported an accuracy of 99.39% using RBF kernel of SVM classifier. According to them, this task is the first of its kind that identifies English words and numerals from Gurmukhi script. Dataset of 26500 samples comprising 265 Tamil offline city names has been developed by Thadchanamoorthy *et al.* [7] and they have also proposed a recognition scheme.

Nehra *et al.* [8] have developed a dataset for offline handwritten characters with modifiers in Hindi language. The database consists of more than 23000 images of handwritten characters comprising consonants and vowels written by around 1500 writers. According to them, there is no such kind of dataset exists for characters with modifiers handwritten in Devanagari script. Dasgupta *et al.* [9] developed a segmentation free method for recognition of offline handwritten cursive words. They have extracted directional features from the word images and Support Vector Machine (SVM) is employed as a classifier. According to them, it is for the first time that Arnold transformation has been employed for extraction of directional features. They tested the method on CENPARMI database with an accuracy of 87.19%. Khemiri *et al.* [10] presented a system for recognition of offline words handwritten in Arabic script using a Bayesian approach. They have considered distinct structural features from the image of the word. For experiments, they have considered IFN/ENIT database and reported the highest rate of 90.02% using Horizontal and Vertical Hidden Markov Model.

In order to avoid character segmentation problems in scripts, Roy *et al.* [11] proposed HMM based holistic approach with a combination of PHOG (Pyramid Histogram of Oriented Gradient) feature for the identification of words handwritten in Bangla and Devanagari script. The proposed approach segments the word image into three zones horizontally, such as upper, middle and lower zones. Then, HMM is employed for recognition of the middle zone and SVM classifier for recognition of modifiers in upper and lower zones. Finally, recognition of a word is obtained by integrating the zone-wise results on the database containing 17,091 word samples of Bangla script with accuracy of 92.89% and 16,128 word samples of Devanagari script with accuracy of 94.51% with top 5 choices, respectively. Dhiman and Lehal [12] presented a comparative analysis of performance at word level for Gurmukhi OCR. They have employed Discrete Cosine Transform (DCT) and Gabor filter as feature extraction techniques to obtain the features from machine printed images. For recognition purpose, k-NN (k-Nearest Neighbour) classifier has been employed. For training the classifier, 1600 samples have been taken. Based on Gabor filter, k-NN classifier reported 92.62% accuracy and using DCT, k-NN reported 96.99% accuracy.

Mukherjee *et al.* [13] developed a novel assignment model of visual words for depicting an image patch including a penalty term for measuring image/patch dissimilarity. Experiments are conducted on publicly accessible COIL-100 image database which shows the higher level performance of the considered content-based image retrieval (CBIR) method as compared to state-of-the-art approaches. Gowda *et al.* [14] developed an offline recognition system for Kannada handwritten words. For extracting the features, Locality Preserving Projections (LPP) method has been employed and SVM has been employed as a classifier. They tested the system on a database containing 30 districts of Karnataka collected from 20 people and reported 80% average rate of recognition. Gupta *et al.* [15] presented a hybrid classifier model for offline recognition of handwritten words using segmentation free approach. They have considered two handmade features, namely, Arnold transform-based features and oriented curvature-based feature and single machine made feature using DCNN (Deep

Convolution Neural Network). Three SVM classifiers have been utilized to recognize these three features whose outputs are then combined, in order to recognize the word. For evaluation purpose, they have considered three databases, namely, CENPARMI database, IAM database and ISIHWD database and reported a recognition accuracy of 97.16% on ISIHWD database.

In order to resolve the problem of text recognition in scripts that are having less training data, Bhunia *et al.* [16] proposed a cross language framework for words' recognition and in order to spot Indic scripts based on zone-wise character mapping approach where training is done on large dataset of one script and testing is performed on other scripts that are having comparatively lower samples. In order to compute the similarity between two scripts, the entropy of script similarity score is used. They have considered three Indic scripts, namely, Bangla comprising 11,253 words, Devanagari comprising 10,667 words and Gurumukhi comprising 9,243 words as training data, respectively. They have reported higher script similarity index between Bangla and Devanagari as compared to Bangla and Gurumukhi scripts. To the best of their knowledge, this work is the first kind of its type.

3 Gurmukhi Script and Description of Data Set

Gurmukhi script is utilized for composing text in Punjabi language. The term Gurmukhi has been commonly translated as "from the mouth of the Guru" which originates from the old Punjabi word "Guramukhi". The Gurmukhi script contains thirty-two consonants, three vowel bearers, six additional consonants, nine vowel modifiers, three auxiliary signs and three half characters. This script is written from left to right. This script is independent of case sensitivity. The majority of the characters contain a horizontal line at the upper portion and the characters of words are attached mostly in this line called headline. The proposed dataset named as HWR-Gurmukhi_Postal_1.0 has 100 different classes representing 100 unique city names of India. These 100 different words are written by 40 different writers where each writer writes each word 10 times, resulting in total 40,000 words as described in Table 1. These 100 different classes are organized in 100 different folders, namely C1, C2, C3 ...., C100. Total number of samples is 400 in each class. In each category of these 100 classes, training dataset and testing dataset contain 70% and 30% data, respectively.

Table 1. Dataset description

Dataset	Number of writers	Number of times	Number of classes	Number of training sample	Number of testing sample	Total samples
HWR-Gurmukhi_Postal_1.0	40	10	100	28000	12000	40000

The proposed dataset has been created by going through following stages:

A. *Data Collection*

In order to create dataset of Gurmukhi handwritten words, an empty sheet of paper of A4 size has been used. In order to write words on paper, a sample paper had been given to the writers. A single paper contains 50 words, so 2 sample papers were given to the writers containing 100 words. As each writer has to write each word 10 times so each writer generates 20 pages containing 1000 words. To provide the extreme syntactic variations, 40 writers have been considered from different age classes, professional and educational qualifications. The dataset has been collected from different classes of writers like students of schools and colleges, employees of government offices and natives of various public places. Because the person's handwriting sometimes gets affected by the emotions, circumstances and environment. A sample of each category of classes contained in the dataset is shown in Fig. 1.

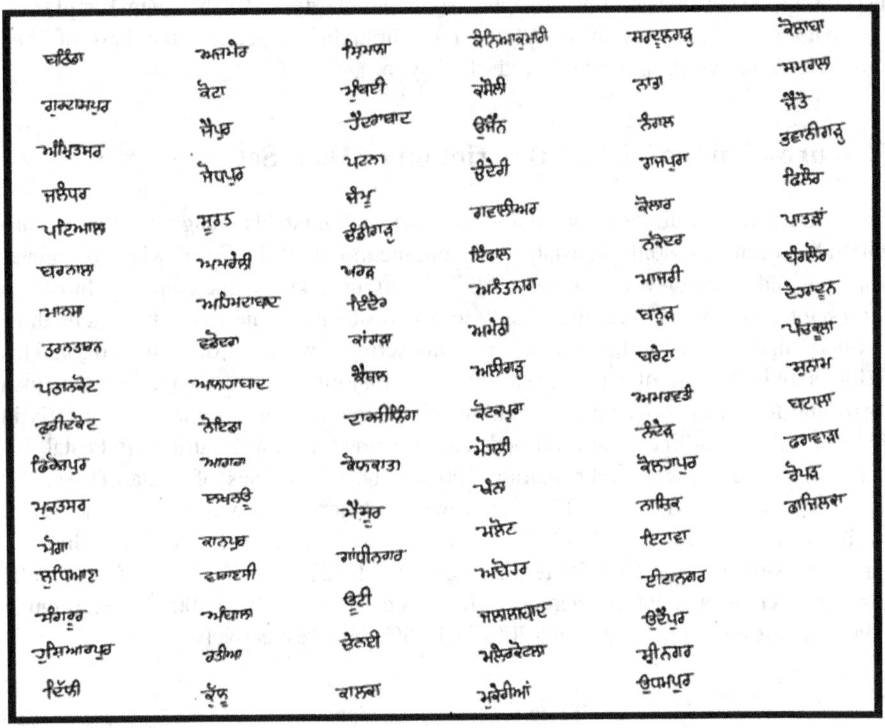

Fig. 1. A sample of each class contained in the dataset

B. *Digitization and Pre-processing*

For the digitization of collected data, text sheets of paper were scanned by using a scanner at 300 dpi and scanned images were saved in a.jpeg image format. Pre-processing consists of a sequence of operations applied on a digital image obtained through the digitization process. Pre-processing normally includes binarization, normalization and thinning operations. For the proposed dataset, we have applied only binarization and normalization process. In binarization, the binary form of the image is obtained containing black and white pixels. For this purpose, the threshold constant is set between higher and lower values which correspond to white and black, respectively. After binarization, we have sliced the words one by one from the binarized image. In order to remove extra white space surrounding the words, sliced words have been cropped. Normalization process is used for normalizing the size of words into uniformity. In the proposed dataset, we have normalized the word image into a window of size 256×64. The complete set of normalized words is kept in the dataset in the.bmp image format. A few samples of the dataset written by three different writers (W1, W2, W3) are shown in Table 2.

Table 2. A few samples of handwritten city names in Gurmukhi script

Script Word	W1	W2	W3
ਬਠਿੰਡਾ			
ਅਜਮੇਰ			
ਸ਼ਿਮਲਾ			
ਮੁੰਬਈ			
ਜੋਧਪੁਰ			

4 Motivation

A benchmark dataset is required for the development of an efficient and reliable postal automation system. Unfortunately, no comprehensive benchmark dataset exists for handwritten Gurmukhi document recognition research. The proposed paper is an effort in this direction. The proposed dataset will be very helpful for validation of recognition algorithms for handwritten text. It can be utilized for cross validation by splitting it as training and testing dataset. This dataset has been made available publicly for researchers so that they can test their proposed techniques on the benchmark dataset without creating a new dataset for Gurmukhi script.

5 Applications of Dataset

A few people compose the destination address portion of a postal document in more than one language. As an example, due to tri-lingual principle of an Indian state, the destination address part of a postal document is usually written in three languages, namely, English, Hindi and the state official language. Owing to the fact of India's multi-lingual and muti-script behaviour, developing a system regarding postal automation is more difficult as compared to other countries. Till now, no postal automation system exists for Gurmukhi script. Thus, the proposed dataset for Gurmukhi script finds its applications in postal automation to identify the address as the dataset contains 100 different city names of India in Punjabi language. In addition, the other application areas of the handwritten word dataset are identification of writer's handwriting, signature verification, recognition of historical documents, form processing in administration, insurance offices etc.

6 Inference

In the proposed paper, we have introduced a dataset for offline handwritten Gurmukhi postal automation at https://sites.google.com/view/gurmukhi-benchmark/home/word-level-gurmukhi-dataset. Till now, no standardized dataset is available for Gurmukhi script, so comparison between existing techniques for Gurmukhi city name recognition is not possible. Thus, the effort of introducing benchmark dataset for Gurmukhi script will be fruitful in comparing the existing techniques and proposed techniques by various scholars in the future. This benchmark dataset will also provide a contribution to boosting the research in the area of offline handwritten Gurmukhi script recognition. In future, the dataset can be expanded to develop a complete corpus of handwritten Gurmukhi city names and lines that will be proved useful for benchmarking of handwritten segmentation algorithms.

Conflict of Interest. Authors have no conflict of interest.

References

1. Mahadevan, U., Srihari, S.N.: Parsing and recognition of city, state, and ZIP codes in handwritten addresses. In: Proceedings of 5th International Conference on Document Analysis and Recognition (ICDAR), pp. 325–328 (1999)
2. Liu, C.-L., Koga, M., Fujisawa, H.: Lexicon-driven segmentation and recognition of handwritten character strings for Japanese address reading. IEEE Trans. Pattern Anal. Mach. Intell. **24**(11), 1425–1437 (2002)
3. Alaei, A., Nagabhushan, P., Pal, U.: A benchmark Kannada handwritten document dataset and its segmentation. In: Proceedings of the 2011 IEEE International Conference on Document Analysis and Recognition (ICDAR), pp. 141–145 (2011)
4. Pal, U., Roy, K., Kimura, F.: A lexicon-driven handwritten city name recognition scheme for Indian postal automation. IEICE Trans. Inf. Syst. **92**(5), 1146–1158 (2009)

5. Pal, U., Roy, R.K., Kimura, F.; Multi-lingual city name recognition for Indian postal automation. In: Proceedings of International Conference on Frontiers in Handwriting Recognition, pp. 169–173 (2012)
6. Rani, R., Dhir, R., Lehal, G.S.: Modified Gabor feature extraction method for word level script identification - experimentation with Gurumukhi and English scripts. Int. J. Signal Process. Image Process. Pattern Recogn. **6**(5), 25–38 (2013)
7. Thadchanamoorthy, S., Kodikara, N.D., Premaretne, H.L.: Tamil handwritten city name database development and recognition for postal automation. In: Proceedings of the 12th International Conference on Document Analysis and Recognition, pp. 793–797 (2013)
8. Nehra, M.S., Nain, N., Ahmed, M.: Handwritten Devanagari script database development for off-line Hindi character with Matra (modifiers). In: Proceedings of the International Conference on Recent Cognizance in Wireless Communication & Image Processing, pp. 233–240 (2016)
9. Dasgupta, J., Bhattacharya, K., Chanda, B.: A holistic approach for Off-line handwritten cursive word recognition using directional feature based on Arnold transform. Pattern Recogn. Lett. **79**, 73–79 (2016)
10. Khemiri, A., Echi, A.K., Belaid, A., Elloumi, M.: A system for off-line Arabic handwritten word recognition based on bayesian approach. In: Proceedings of the 15th International Conference on Frontiers in Handwriting Recognition, pp. 560–565 (2016)
11. Roy, P.P., Bhunia, A.K., Das, A., Dey, P., Pal, U.: HMM-based Indic handwritten word recognition using zone segmentation. Pattern Recogn. **60**, 1057–1075 (2016)
12. Dhiman, S., Lehal, G.S.: Performance comparison of Gurmukhi script: k-NN classifier with DCT and Gabor filter. Int. J. Adv. Res. Comput. Sci. **8**(5), 762–764 (2017)
13. Mukherjee, A., Chakraborty, S., Sil, J., Chowdhury, A.S.: A novel visual word assignment model for content-based image retrieval. In: Proceedings of the International Conference on Computer Vision and Image Processing, pp. 79–87 (2017)
14. Gowda, P.K., Chethan, S., Harsha, J., Rakesh, J., Tanushree, K.N.: Offline Kannada handwritten word recognition using locality preserving projections (LPP). Int. J. Innovative Res. Comput. Commun. Eng. **5**(5), 9955–9960 (2017)
15. Gupta, J.D., Samanta, S., Chanda, B.: Ensemble classifier-based off-line handwritten word recognition system in holistic approach. IET Image Process. **12**(8), 1467–1474 (2018)
16. Bhunia, A.K., Roy, P.P., Mohta, A., Pal, U.: Cross-language framework for word recognition and spotting of Indic scripts. Pattern Recogn. **79**, 12–31 (2018)

Author Index

Printed in the United States
By Bookmasters